Contents

Introductory Remarks

This book provides a detailed insight into the innovative work being undertaken by the Cardiff Option 2 programme, which provides time limited intensive interventions with families in crisis. It sets out very practical examples of how such work can be undertaken and encourages professionals to reflect on different models of intervention. An evidence informed approach in undertaking assessments, and in working with children and their families, requires practitioners to analyse carefully their information and to apply that information in ways which produce positive outcomes. The work undertaken by the Option 2 programme provides an example of one of the approaches, which may be considered in working with children and families in crisis. This book provides readers with detailed and positive information, which will allow them to draw out those lessons which might be applied in their own work.

Jane Hutt AM
Minister for Health and Social Services, Welsh Assembly

Dedication

To all the families and individuals who invited me into their homes and their lives, who told me of their dreams for the future, who learned alongside me, laughed, and cried with me and who reminded me each day that this life is about becoming more than you are today. Thanks Sally, Lawrence, Jodie, Elisabeth, Thomas, Jessica, Michael, Rebecca, Penny, Katy, Louis, Christian, Charmaine, Wendy, Khalid, Christine, Mark, Matthew, Tina, Jean, Robert, Clifford, Mercedes, Carmen, Keanu, Katherine, Paul, Joseph, Sean, Ryan, Wanda, Soraya, Kai, Leighla, Jordan, Katherine, Michael, Semina, Owen, Malcolm, Leanne, Cameron, Keanna, Roxanne, Darren, Simone, Raoul, Zenon, Maia, Emma, Jack, Joanne, Jessica, Linda, Ashely, Charlotte, Marianne, Stephanie, Christina, Kevin, Lauren, Alana, Callum, Tracey, Jack, Nina, Tracey, John, John, Kim, Holly, Claire, David, Jack, Katie, Jade, Tracey, Paula, Keion, Kerry, Ashley, Christian, Chloe, Tiegan, Amanda, Suzanne, Daniel, Rebecca, Bethan, Julie, Joshua, Andrew, Ali, Elizabeth, Elin, Sian, John, Gabrielle, Lucinda, Dean, Julie, Dean, Lisa, Freddie, Charlotte, Connor, Gail, Nicholas, Lynne, Patrick, Tracey, Stephen, Richard, Samantha, Lucia, Rachel, Mark, Chantelle, Cherelle, Dara, Rajpal, Aska, Karam, Lakhveer, Ghena, Azadi and all those yet to come.

> *If you want to build a ship, then don't drum up men to gather wood, give orders, and divide the work.*
> *Rather, teach them to yearn for the far and endless sea.*
> *As for the future, your task is not to foresee it, but to enable it.*

From *The Wisdom of the Sands* by Antoine de Saint-Exupery

Who This Book is for

Whatever setting you work in as a health or welfare worker, you will eventually find yourself becoming concerned about the impact of an individual's difficulty on their family and the ability of the family to support the individual. The tools and ideas in this book will be useful to a wide range of workers who recognise the impact of the individual on the family and accept the importance of the cohesion of those families to all the individuals involved. This includes:

- mental health workers
- counsellors
- substance misuse workers
- family centre staff
- family support teams
- crisis intervention teams
- social workers of all disciplines
- probation officers and members of youth offending teams

. . . and others whose work brings them into contact with families in difficulty. All will find tools here to help them to support those families and promote their resilience. This book, with a few minor alterations, could equally have been called *Building Confidence and Self Esteem in Families*.

We use this model at our projects in South Wales, specifically with families where there are parental substance misuse and serious child protection concerns. Child protection is part of the wide spectrum of work with families and is not only carried out by child protection workers but firstly by families and also by professionals from other fields. Whichever category you fall into, if you work with families in difficulty, then I believe you will find useful interventions in this book.

About the Author

Working in a fieldwork team sometimes made me feel like an underdog and although service users felt like I had all the power, I didn't feel like I had any at all and I struggled with those feelings of powerlessness.

Over a period of time I realised that to do the things I really wanted to do as a social worker I didn't need any power. I had never wanted to police or control people. What I really wanted to do was to help people find their own power and be autonomous, the power to keep themselves and their families safe, to make good decisions, to explore who they really are, to be who they want to be and yet rub along with the rest of the world.

We can be very specific and talk about how we can help stressed parents to improve their parenting or stop drinking or deal with their anger, but such improvements are really the side effects of giving people the opportunity to stop reacting and dream for a moment. When people create goals based upon their visions of a possible better future, they develop a target to aim for and a belief in their ability to achieve their goals and create that future. Truly not everything that is dreamed comes to fruition but nothing happens that has not first been dreamed or created in the imagination.

When I decided to give up the struggle for power, suddenly as well as realising that I already had all the power I ever needed, I knew what I needed to do with my life. Through good luck or through synchronicity I have been given the opportunities I needed and have been taught by some truly inspirational people.

Acknowledgements

I want to thank Doug and Soledad, practitioners in the USA, for teaching me how to work with families. Dr Jill Kinney for allowing me to reproduce some of her pioneering work. Rhoda Emlyn-Jones for fighting for so hard and so long to bring this service to the UK, for bringing me together with my teachers and for allowing me to explore my potential. I must of course thank the substance misuse branch of The National Assembly of Wales, and the Cardiff and Vale Community Safety Partnership who had the foresight and creativity to fund and support the Option 2 project in Cardiff and The Vale of Glamorgan. Thanks to Dr Amanda Bremble, who worked with me in the Spring of 2000 to set up what was then a unique project in the UK. Thanks to Option 2 workers past and present who inspire me, accept my eccentricities, give me the space to write and who supported me in this project; Kendal and Amanda, Debbie, Cheryl, Mandy and Anthony. I also must thank the Brief Therapy Practice in London for their notes used in the section on Brief Therapy. Anthony Lewis, Brief Therapist and Trainer for help with the section on SFBT and The Community Alcohol and Drug Team in Cardiff who provide world class training and information on Motivational Interviewing. Thanks and my deepest love must go to my wife and life partner Kate who is a real writer.

Any errors or omissions are mine alone, any glories belong to all the people who put this into practice, families and workers. This book draws from a variety of sources collected over a number of years, many of the sources now untraceable. If I have used your work, please let me know and I will make what effort I am able to redress this.

Mark Hamer, Cardiff, August 2004

Foreword

Families in need often require the close co-operation of a wide range of expertise from a range of organisations. Sometimes it appears as if the systems cannot work effectively together to give children and families the service they need at the time that they need it.

Throughout my time as a child care social worker and since, developing alcohol and drug services in the community, I was aware of the failings in all our systems. With the best will in the world we couldn't meet the needs appropriately. We longed to provide a more effective service.

We needed a service that was accessible, intensive, transparent and ready, willing and able to respond to each individual family at the moment of crisis.

Jill Kinney's work developing Homebuilders in America provided the inspiration. We adopted the principles and the approach and adapted it to fit our Welsh context. It took many years to establish the funding to pilot Option 2 in Cardiff and expand into Barry and the Vale of Glamorgan two years later, so it is very heartening now to see the impact of our small but significant service on the lives of the children and families who have used it.

It is with great pleasure and some awe that I commend Mark's excellent work. He has balanced his skills and energy to focus upon his family work and his writing and been able to bring this successful approach to a much wider audience.

The Option 2 team are highly skilled and committed; my role is to ensure that the organisational structure that surrounds them mirrors our service principles and working conditions must focus on releasing creativity and resources and building on resilience. Successful services depend upon successful models and skilled, committed staff, but the management approach and organisational culture is also crucial.

There are many resourceful professionals out there and many resourceful families. We need to bring them together in services that enable them to succeed.

I cannot emphasise enough my respect for the Option 2 therapists, past and present, and for all the families who have challenged and changed their lives in the most difficult circumstances.

Most children, not all, but most, do not ask us to save them from their families, they ask us to help their families keep each other safe. If children can grow up safely in the place they want to be we have a duty to do all we can to help them achieve that.

The method and approach outlined in this book is proving very effective and I hope will be of interest to managers and practitioners throughout the UK.

Rhoda Emlyn-Jones. Service Manager

Introduction

They themselves are the makers of themselves . . . as a man thinketh, so he is.

James Allen, *As a Man Thinketh* (1864–1912)

Part One of this manual is a simple list of principles that we feel are important to work with families. Part Two looks at how we structure a brief solution focussed intervention in our projects in South Wales, and from Part Three onwards the manual contains tools and concepts that anybody working with families can use to the benefit of their clients.

Seen as a whole, this is a model of a time-limited intervention for families in crisis. It is based on the model we use in Cardiff with families where child protection social workers are seriously considering the need to remove the children. This intervention provides another option for some of those families so we named our service *Option 2*. Our aim is to prevent accommodation of those children, using a solution focussed approach to change risk behaviour in those families. We provide a different way of dealing with child protection work, one which we feel is to the benefit of children, families and workers.

This intervention style is about the refocussing of child care practice, about intervening at an earlier stage and focussing on prevention before protection becomes necessary. The recent green paper, 'every child matters' (2003), and the report from the Dartington Social Research Unit 'Refocussing Children's Services Towards Prevention: Lessons from the literature' (2004), will be seen to support practically everything in this book, indeed this manual could be seen as a way to implement many of the recommendations in those papers.

Practitioners will read about holistic social work, which uses well researched and established tools and ideas for assessing and working therapeutically with families. You will also read about some unusual but practical service strategies that support our work and help us to provide a service that families find useful.

This intervention is based on a way of working with childcare cases which originated in the USA where they call it 'Homebuilders' (Kinney, Haapala and Booth, 1991). While travelling in the USA my manager, Rhoda Emlyn-Jones, met one of the originators, Jill Kinney, and seeing it in action was inspired to bring it to the UK where we adapted the model to work in a British context. In 2001 we won the Community Care Award for Child Protection and have been featured in the local and national media for our pioneering work in child protection. In the early days we could find nobody else using this model in the UK, so we offered training to practitioners from across the UK and now we do not feel so alone.

We help struggling families to change for the better, to improve their lives and to keep children in the families to which they belong. The families we work with are often trying to cope with drug or alcohol misuse, depression, self-harm, domestic violence, physical, social and emotional poverty, poor coping skills, uninformed parenting, insecurity, uncertainty, fear and isolation. It is a fundamental belief of ours that people are doing the best they can with what they know, the vital process of life for all of us is about growth, we are all in the process of becoming. Like Carl Rogers (1961) I believe that people are striving to heal themselves. When we, as workers for the community, use the right communication skills to give people new ways of doing things, their lives improve. We know their lives improve because they tell us that and because we and others can see them coping better.

The power for change resides in the family and we help people to access that power by enabling them to feel confident and important enough to take control and to create some clear goals and solutions. When you pay attention to what people are capable of doing and what they have succeeded in doing in the past, people automatically feel stronger and more competent and more motivated to make positive changes in their lives.

This solution building paradigm allows workers to interview and investigate in ways which leave the client feeling better off for having had contact with them. Not only do they feel better but they think and behave differently. This kind of motivational, empowering work helps people to feel respected and respectable, more in control, more able to effect change and more motivated. People become more effective.

Social work can be a wonderful job. To the people we work with, what we do matters. I can look back on my career and see families whose lives have been changed for the better, lives have been saved, children have avoided years of abuse, families have grown up with hope, people have got educated, got employed and got off drugs because of what I did with them. Many of us come to this profession with the belief that everybody at some time or other has a difficult time and needs help. Social workers are one of society's collective responses to the need to provide professional services to help people through those times. It is a human job about human beings, a job built on relationships. At its best it is a job that allows you to be creative, to help others, to experience other people's lives, to have a positive and valid role in the world, to protect the weak and vulnerable and to change people's lives for the better.

Yet so often when I was a field social worker, I felt jammed into fulfilling a role that I hadn't asked for and ended up changing people's lives for the worse. I went home angry, depressed and frustrated because although I had the belief the family could change and the children could be protected, and I had the desire to do the work, I did not have the tools, the time or the autonomy to make a positive difference. The way I had to work affected and damaged my life. I was not alone; McMahon (1988) vividly described social workers suffering from negative physical reactions that include nausea, sickness, depression, nightmares and ulcers; he wrote that 'their bodies were wearing out because of the way they had to do their work'.

Mistrust is a powerful factor in the relationship between professionals and the organisation they serve. The relationship between client, worker and employer is a hierarchical one. Trust needs to start at the top and trickle down. It is the role of employers to ensure that their workers feel respected, trusted and supported. If workers do not feel trusted it is inevitable that mistrust will become a factor in the relationship between worker and client no matter how professional workers may be. In practice this results in the whole organisation from the top down developing a culture of mistrust and hence fear and a problem focus.

Workers, teams and organisations who have a problem focus fail to see solutions and fail to promote positive outcomes, instead they become fixated on trying to avoid negative ones. With a problem focussed approach, failure is so easy to observe and measure whilst success is elusive, mistrusted when we see it and impossible to pin down with the tools that are available to us. The outcome is that clients end up in the system for years, decisions are made to protect children rather than support families and children are accommodated.

When support is offered to families it is often problematic. The concept of 'support' itself is a functional double-edged sword that is often used to label families that refuse to accept it. Families rarely want to fail and if they found support truly supportive, they would use it. I am sure many of us have worked with clients who have had imposed on them massive numbers of services that they find more stressful than useful but accept because they know the risks of being labelled as 'refusing services'.

We often come across the word 'support' in reports or Case Conferences, sometimes it goes along the lines of, 'despite all the support we have been offering to Mr and Mrs Whotsit, they continue to be unable to provide adequate parenting . . . etc. etc.' This 'support' can include such a wide variety of interventions as to make the term meaningless. For example it could include a simple expression of empathy, a telling off, the accommodation of a child, a fortnightly half hour visit or something drawn from the social workers 'menu' of available resources such as nursery facilities, childminding, parenting groups, Core Groups and so on. It is a meaningless catch-all phrase that workers currently use to describe a variety of activities which may be more or less useful or supportive to a family. The real effect of these different types of support in terms of family functioning are very rarely evaluated.

I believe that the single most common reason for lack of success in social work is because there are no clear goals and without clear goals there is no possibility of evaluation. Evaluation must be weaved into the planning of any service, it should be part of the planning and setting of goals and part of the communication style workers use.

What is really supportive is listening to families and finding out what people really feel they need. It is an axiom of solution focussed brief therapy that clients are always trying to co-operate with us, they are trying to tell us what they need if only we will listen sensitively to them.

Cooper and Hetherington (2003) argue that childcare professionals work in defensive organisations that do not encourage trust at any level. They argue that years and years of increasing bureaucracy and risk aversion have led us into a dead end resulting in poor staff morale and institutionally abused families. The risk avoidance culture we work in creates a cynical view of clients which creates a self-fulfilling prophecy: Our cynicism makes clients dishonest and we become more cynical.

I could argue here and make a plea for organisations to change the way they do things, to trust workers more and give them more professional autonomy and responsibility, to focus on prevention, to listen to clients. To measure outcomes instead of inputs. To be concerned with quality and effectiveness of work instead of quantity of activity, for services to be needs led rather than service led, all recommendations from the Climbie enquiry. But I am a pragmatist and no Pollyanna. I know that individuals alone cannot make organisations change, especially when those individuals and their organisations are careworn and struggling. When such individuals express their feelings, their passion is often seen as a symptom of their underlying problem and their dissent becomes pathologised. There is really no point demanding that those who have power over you respect you as an individual and try better ways of doing things unless, that is, you really feel that there is not enough disappointment in your life. The system you work in may resemble a lumbering ego-ridden dugong with politicians hanging from every teat. It needs a lot of pressure from above to make it even think about changing direction, and then it will make excuses for years before finally snorting like a teenager and flapping a token flipper in vaguely the right direction. It can't help it, that is the nature of systems. It is no surprise that clients mistrust the system and our part in it.

Real social change is always driven from the bottom by people who are willing to challenge the status quo and break new ground. The time honoured way of dealing with such scenarios is to think global and act local. I am making the assumption that you feel the need to do things differently. Maybe you have the authority and finances to set up a new resource or maybe you can change the way you work as an individual or perhaps you are looking to try a few different tools. You can be an individual to your clients and not just a part of a system that they fear. You can be a real social worker, helping the weak to deal with the powerful. Fantasise (if you have to) about how it could be and do your best to do your best. The lives you touch will be better for it.

Think for a moment what your clients would like out of you. If you are having trouble, just think what you would like out of your employer. After all you are part of that system. You might come up with a list something like this:

- Communication

- Trust

- Honesty

- Help and support

- Understanding

- Openness

- Respect

- Fairness

- Empowerment

- Freedom

- Power

- More focus on solutions rather than problems

- Being treated as an individual rather than a problem

This way of working offers all of those things. It offers real support that families can use to change for the better. It offers the organisation and the practitioner a way of working that is effective. It offers you as an individual a way of working within an organisation and provide families with real opportunities. This way of organising services has been adopted by a number of local authorities who have been on our training courses (see useful contacts right at the end of this manual).

Families speaking

Our clients respond positively to what we do. These comments are just a few of those made by adults and children we have worked with over the years. They are drawn from our evaluation process and are kept on file at our office in Cardiff.

[Worker] listened, observed and knew where I was coming from, he never pressurised me and [he] made me feel able to talk openly, [he] did more for me than anyone in 7 years of therapy.

Made me back to the real person I am.

Helped me and the children to play together again.

[The worker] was a friend – still is – caring and came into my life when I needed a human like her.

Got us back together as a family.

[He] knows who I am in life and what my goals are.

They need more people like [this].

Made us feel warm and that we were someone . . . made us laugh again with each other and not at each other.

They listen . . . they work with us, not against us.

I am glad to have had [worker] as I probably wouldn't have got where I am now and getting further ahead to what I want in life.

Has given me hope.

[worker] is brill and has done a lot for me, many thanks, in a way I met a new friend. Nice one.

. . . has been extremely helpful at putting back the perspective in my family life. It has helped me to deal positively with the past and to get control for our future. It has helped me to view myself and my role as a parent in a much more positive light.

I could not explain how [worker] has helped us as a family. [worker] is worth their weight in gold.

I can't see how it can be improved.

I was at crisis point, nobody was listening to me. I was being judged by the people paid to support me and had very little confidence and self esteem left. I constantly made bad decisions because I was so frustrated with how I was being treated. Now people listen to me, I have a good positive friendships, a beautiful relationship with my son and I feel confident in making the right decisions and the right steps to keep myself and my son safe.

I have achieved so much, my son had behavioural problems due to the violence he has seen – he is a changed boy, he again listens to me and has a clear routine.

I can budget properly now.

I can do the creative things that I enjoy. I can see the positive in every situation and identify my feelings.

The most helpful person we have had in the last six months.

Made us realise our family is important. Taught us the values of loving and most important kept our family together.

Made us feel like a proper family.

Gave us inspiration toward our future.

Reminded me of the person that I really am.

I could talk things over which happened in my past and I found it so difficult to talk about, this happened 30+ years ago, it was good to get it off my chest.

Gave us our lives back . . . gave us hope and a reason to fight.

I feel happy, you know the proper happy from inside.

CHAPTER 1

Guiding Principles

The measure of a man is how he treats someone who can do him no good.

Anon

Our guiding principles form the foundation on which our work with families is built. From these ideas come the tools and the core skills that we use every day.

We can't tell if it is hopeless

- We do not know which families we can be successful with until we try.

- If **we** feel hopeless, we can't help the client and we can't instil hope in the client.

It is our job to motivate clients and instil hope

- We work to instil hope by building on existing, possibly hidden strengths.

- People do not resolve problems by drawing on their deficits; they do it by drawing on their strengths and resources.

- We cannot make clients change; clients will change or not change depending on the resources upon which they can draw.

- When we feel hopeful we can point out their past success and fan the flames of hope.

Clients are our partners

- They are people like us.

- We share resources and accept clients as experts on their own situation.

- The process is therapeutic and draws out strengths and resources the client has.

Sometimes workers can make life worse for families

- By providing inappropriate services, or services people are not ready for.

- By imposing services just because we have them or because we want somebody to monitor the family for us.

- By ignoring existing strengths and expertise.

- By feeling that there is no hope.

- By ignoring the values specific to this family. We work with the person rather than the problem.

- By interfering with and damaging the 'good' parts of family life, e.g. too many different people visiting can mean that families miss out on 'normal' activities together.

We must guard against our tendency to remake families and clients into our own ideal image of a family or parent

- Find out who they are, what they believe, what are their strengths, proudest moments, achievements, spiritual beliefs.

- We are all different and my families' lovely relaxing day is your boring nightmare.

- What are the real and present issues for the individuals in this family? Leave your own moral judgements, gut reactions and 'common sense' at home.

On the whole, people are doing the best they can with what they know

- Few people want to harm their children and when they do, most regret it.

- Sometimes their skills and resources only go so far.

- Sometimes people do not realise that their behaviour is harmful to their children. Confronting this head on by just telling them will create resistance.

We can change behaviour without understanding the why of the behaviour

- By providing extra resources, skills and tools. We teach new skills and coping mechanisms.

- It is not necessary to know 'why' to effect real change.

- The 'why' is often unknowable.

- Problems do not necessarily represent underlying pathology. They are usually just things that the client wants to do without.

- We focus on the clients presenting problems, looking at the here and now. History may hold valuable lessons but care must be taken not to confuse it with the present.

It is our basic job to empower clients

We work 'with', not 'to'. It is the task of the worker to determine the client's unique way of moving forward and co-operating with the work.

- We talk about what they want to talk about.

- We meet when and where they want to meet.

We can help the whole family to make changes even if the whole family does not work with us

- Systems approach-working with one family member will create a 'snowball effect'.

- We can work with family members who are not physically there, one person's behaviour affects another person's behaviour.

- Teach one member something useful and others will want to learn them too, e.g. how to relax.

The whole family is our client

- Work with individuals, families and friendship groups, listen to people singly and in groups.

We must pause and plan

- Observe and learn, hypothesise, test and reformulate.

Our role is to help families to provide a safe and secure home for the children

We like to have a copy of these principles up on the office wall. Sometimes it helps to be reminded of basics when dealing with a complicated issue or family.

- We can't tell if it is hopeless.

- It is our job to motivate clients and instil hope.

- Clients are our partners.

- Sometimes workers can make life worse for families.

- We must guard against our tendency to remake families and clients into our own ideal image of a family or parent.

- On the whole, people are doing the best they can with what they know.

- We can change behaviour without understanding the why of the behaviour.

- It is our basic job to empower clients.

- We can help the whole family to make changes even if the whole family does not work with us.

- The whole family is our client.

- We must pause and plan.

- Our role is to help families to provide a safe and secure home for the children.

CHAPTER 2

An Overview of the 'Option 2' Model

Too often we underestimate the power of a touch, a smile, a kind word, a listening ear, a compliment or the smallest act of caring, all of which have the potential to turn a life around.

Leo Buscaglia (1924–1988)

Availability

In this section I want to look at some of the unusual strategies we use in Cardiff. One challenging aspect of this may be the workers availability to clients. We set our service up from scratch and we designed it to be as useful as possible to service users, that meant using some unusual strategies which mostly relate to being available for clients when they wanted us. We were able to employ people who were from the outset aware of what we were going to be asking of them.

It is important to families that we are able to give them as much time as they need without us having to rush off to another appointment or looking at our watches and not paying attention to them. Our workers only work with two families at any one time so that they can be available to families for as long as is useful. The first few days of the intervention are usually quite intense so we stagger our intake so that therapists are not taking two families on at the same time.

We work when it is suitable for the client, usually about five days a week for two to three hours at a time. We focus clearly upon the clients needs and so we make our appointments for when it suits them. That includes evenings, holidays and weekends if that is what they will find helpful.

Trouble has no timetable and we want to be available to use any 'teachable moments' that occur. So we are accessible to clients for 24 hours a day. Each worker is provided with a mobile telephone and the number is given to the client so that the worker may be contacted in an emergency for the duration of the intervention. We believe that if we are available at the right time we can help the family to learn how to deal with whatever crisis has presented itself.

In practice we find that most clients respect our privacy and need for a break. In five years of doing this I have only had two unplanned night time call outs. Most people will save it for the next day knowing that I will be visiting. Some will telephone asking for advice, others will want to talk over a difficult situation and a very small number will really need you to visit. Most clients respect boundaries and do not call in the evenings, weekends or bank holidays.

We provide our services in the client's natural environment. That means we usually work in their homes and community, the supermarket, the gym, the beach, the park or anywhere else the client may feel comfortable. We work with whoever is there when we visit, that may be relatives, friends, parents, children or grandparents. That way we can experience people behaving more naturally, in context and be present during 'teachable moments'.

We do not keep a waiting list. If a family is in crisis (see next section) then they need help immediately before it all boils out of anybody's control. So we provide an immediate response to crisis. Following referral we make first contact with families within 24 hours. If the service is full, all the workers are at capacity, then we do not offer a service.

The Option 2 intervention is short and intense. We work with families in crisis, when they are at a turning point in their lives. We use this crisis state to develop and encourage new behaviours. We do this for the natural duration of a crisis, 4–6 weeks. We usually spend about 30 hours with each client. That is probably about a years worth of conventional face to face social work, concentrated into a few weeks. Realistically each worker can expect to work with about 12 families in a year. This doesn't sound very many until you consider that each one of those families will have reached some kind of resolution, we will have prevented a number of accommodations and the financial, emotional and social cost that goes along with that. Some cases will be closed, a few will have had children appropriately accommodated, most will have moved from a 'child protection' to a 'child in need' category.

We have a small budget for each client so that we can help to meet basic needs and provide a context that enables clients to engage with a therapeutic intervention.

People often ask about the effect on workers of permanent availability to clients. Wondering about the stresses of knowing that your telephone could ring at any time, and how it feels to have no 'downtime'. Staff who are worn out cannot offer a good service. Alongside the normal management supervision we offer non-managerial clinical supervision and peer group supervision. We trust our workers to manage their energy levels and to tell us how best they would like to do that. Workers, just like clients are individuals and have their own ways of healing and managing themselves, some like to get together and relax, others prefer to spend time alone in the mountains, or to spend time with their own families. A cornerstone of this work is that individuals are unique and have their own ways of doing things, there is no right or wrong way, just 'what works'.

At the end of an intervention there is often a natural break between ending one piece of family work and starting a new one. There are a number of other tasks that need doing, follow up visits with old families, paperwork and other 'housekeeping tasks' to do. When workers are between families they will have their mobile telephones switched off, these are often times of recuperation, reflection and sometimes of celebration.

Crisis intervention

We take referrals from childcare social workers when they are concerned that the risk to children is so great that the removal or registration of the children is a very real consideration.

Such a threat inevitably precipitates a crisis for many families. In a crisis, people's normal coping mechanisms break down and no longer provide the support they once did (Roberts, 1995). They feel angry, hopeless, unable to cope, they lose confidence, their self worth is damaged, they feel that they are failing as parents and as human beings and they often do not understand why they are confused. They realise that how they behave and live their lives has led them to the verge of losing their children.

During this state people are not anchored in their usual routines because those routines are failing them, their beliefs are being challenged, their world view, their dreams of the future are all threatened, often very confused and not knowing what to do or where to turn for help. It is important at this time that appropriate help is available. There is no point a worker telling somebody to change or they will lose their child. Telling a client to change without properly showing them how to change is like a sculptor smashing a stone with a sledgehammer and then expecting the pieces to form a statue of David.

If people are left alone in this extremely vulnerable state without appropriate support or guidance, they will often be extremely distressed and chaotic in private but will try to put on a brave face in public while they try internally to restructure their view of the world and to keep some sense of self-worth intact. To the world all may appear well. Superficially they may appear diffident or uncaring saying things like 'I don't care, just do what you want' and an insensitive worker may feel that the client is happy with, or resigned to losing their child.

At this point people are very open to new ideas, to trying new ways of doing things, to listening to new beliefs. At the point of telling the family that they are considering the need to remove a child, a social worker should also be thinking about a brief solution focussed intervention that will help people to make some real changes. Many belief systems look upon crisis as a learning situation, a natural and maturational time for change. The Chinese ideograph for crisis contains two symbols, one meaning 'danger', the other representing 'opportunity'.

This opportunity to change lasts for between four and six weeks before reaching some form of resolution and the door closes again (Golan, 1972; Roberts, 1990). Individuals in crisis may come out of the other side functioning either at a higher or lower level than before the crisis (Dattilio and Freeman, 2000; Roberts, 1995; Parad and Parad, 1990; Roberts, 1990; Burgess and Baldwin, 1981; Fischer, 1978).

At such a point, families need an intervention. They are open and ready for change and they need help to find out who they are going to become, how they are going to live their lives. There is a substantial body of evidence which argues that the effectiveness of a time limited therapeutic intervention can be indistinguishable from that of long term treatment. Supportive social resources, a dynamic form of treatment and focussed techniques at this time can produce a maximum therapeutic effect (Bloom, 1992; Fischer, 1978; Parad, op cit).

Waiting lists

It has been well known for many years that when clients of any therapeutic service get put on waiting lists, by the time they get a service they no longer want it (Eysenk, 1966). One cynical view is that waiting lists are tools used by clinicians to give clients a chance to sort themselves out. However our clients have gone beyond sorting themselves out and are about to lose their children, their choices have been taken away from them. Crisis Intervention theory tells us that people will adapt to their environment within four to six weeks, there is no point us providing a crisis intervention service after the crisis is over and so we do not have a waiting list.

A structured intervention

Before we look in detail at the tools we use, it may be worth looking at how an intervention is structured and an overview of the elements within that structure. This intervention has a very clear process. We might not use all of the elements outlined here with every client and we may sometimes use them in a different order. The client and their needs drive the process forward. However, a classic intervention looks like this:

Taking the referral

Referral is made by a childcare social worker contacting us in person or by telephone. Taking the referral uses the same complex communication skills that we use with families.

The first thing you will be looking for are the facts – what is happening today. Focussing on the observed behaviours that create risk, the real observed risks and not opinions, stories from the past or what people do not like about the parent's behaviour. You will be using solution focussed language, reflecting both feelings and content and so enabling the referrer to be clear about his concerns.

We then discuss with referrers what they want to see in the way of change, what are the referrers hopes for the future, what practical steps need to be taken, what are their expectations for this family at the end of the intervention. We will want to discuss behaviours that would help to make the children safe. It is important to set some clear goalposts with the referrer, ask them how they would know that things had improved. Those goals for the family need to be realistic, ask them 'how much improved' they feel is realistic.

We collect information and fill in a referral form; we feel that it is important that we fill in the referral form as a result of dialogue with the referrer. Intake is a process of setting clear goalposts so that everybody knows what behaviour is expected and can clearly see when it has been achieved, during the process we are helping the referrer to be clear about their concerns and to think in solution focussed terms.

During this screening process we will refer to the referral criteria (see Appendix section for a flowchart for practitioners and referrers).

Referral criteria

- Children must be at real risk of accommodation or having their names placed on the Child Protection Register.

- Children must be living at home or are to return home within seven days.

- Families must be clearly aware that there is a real risk of their children being removed or having their names placed on the CPR.

- Is the family in crisis?

- Children must have an allocated social worker who will continue to have case responsibility during our intervention.

- The family needs to know that a referral is being made.

We complete a referral form before we decide whether we are going to work with a family or not. That gives us a record of activity that did not necessarily result in work with a family. If we have not got a space to work with a family we still fill in a referral form so we have a measure of unmet need. If the criteria are met and if we have a space, then we will make contact with the family within 24 hours and make an appointment to visit them at the most convenient time for them.

Making contact

Our projects are normally set up in teams of two therapists and a part time admin support worker. Before meeting a client for the first time, a therapist will give the client's details to his or her colleague. This is part of our staff safety system (see Safety policy, Chapter 11).

Our aim when making an initial contact with the family is to see the children and simply to be invited back to talk about how we may work together. At this point we just listen to the client's story.

In the first 72 hours after the referral we work with the family to assess whether they fit the referral criteria. At this point the main question is 'is this family really in crisis and ready to make real changes in the way they live'. It does not matter at this point if the family are not confident in their ability to change. What does matter is that change is important enough. You may want to ask a scaling question:

> *On a scale of one to ten, where one is not at all important and ten is the most important thing in your life right now. How important is it that you work to make things better?*

If they do not feel that it is important to change, then the family may not be in crisis, we need to be able to answer these questions:

- Is this a time of change for them?

- Are they going to change whether we do anything or not?

- Is it possible or likely that things could change for the worse?

- Could time spent with the family, helping them to plan, set goals and learn new skills help them to change for the better?

It is sometimes the case that our early work exploring the issues helps people to realise the critical nature of their situation and they will then become motivated to change. The early stages of the intervention are sometimes characterised by a Motivational Interviewing style of communication and this helps to highlight the reality of the situation.

In the first 72 hours we look at immediate risks with the family. We explore briefly the resources, beliefs and strengths the family has, what behaviour they can change immediately and what practical immediate steps they can take that can overcome these risks and prevent an accommodation. We create a written safety plan which is designed to last for the first few days while we begin work. In essence this is an agreement that describes risk behaviour and is clear about each person's responsibility when risk behaviour happens, safety plans are covered in detail later in part nine of this manual.

Assessment concepts to consider

- Assessment should increase client's self knowledge.

- Assessments should lead directly to activity planning.

- Assessments should be user-friendly.

- Assessment should create understanding of client values and culture.

- Assessment improves a desire to change.

- Assessments should be family friendly with no jargon, and everything making sense to the family.

- Assessments should be a pleasant experience.

- Assessments should identify existing formal services, resources and funding, weight their usefulness to the family's needs and lead to the creation of additional services as required.

- Assessments should identify your own skill training needs.

Inappropriate referrals

The threat of removal or registration is enough to put many families into crisis and feel the urgent need to make changes. For some families that is not the case. Below are some common reasons for a referral being deemed inappropriate within 72 hours:

1   Family does not feel the urgent need to make changes (no sense of crisis).

2   Children are not living at home.

3   There is no case responsible childcare worker.

4   There is no real threat of accommodation or registration.

5   We do not feel that the children can be made be safe during the intervention.

In such instances the referral will not be accepted. Sometimes our involvement may highlight the risks to the point of initiating a crisis. We may then become able to engage the family in a therapeutic process. If the family continues to feel that they do not need to make urgent changes, then further work will be inappropriate as the prospect of change at that point is unlikely. At this point the therapist may decide that the family does not fit the referral criteria and the case may be closed. It may be that another referral will need to be made at a later stage when the reality of the situation has impacted the family and they realise that changes have to be made.

However, during the first three days we work on developing confidence and self esteem, creating a positive vision of the future and goal planning. We may also want to refer some clients on to other agencies at this point. For some families this three day period will itself create some positive change.

We need to be sure during this time that the children can be conditionally safe during the intervention, it helps to use scales. For example on a scale of one to ten where one is 'no risk' and ten is 'severe danger', where would the worker place this family in terms of risk to the children. If we feel that we cannot make the children conditionally safe for the duration of the intervention we would speak to the referrer about our concerns and consider the need to withdraw.

After 72 hours a report is written to the social worker and the family, this explains what has been agreed between the worker and client and whether the intervention will continue for a full four weeks or not. This includes any safety plan that has been devised and any early goals set.

Briefer interventions

An average intervention would involve a worker being with the family for around 30 hours over a four week period.

It may be the case that, once you have engaged with the family, you become aware that there is clear and positive work you can do that will help the family but the work does not warrant a full four week intervention. Alternatively the family do not meet the referral criteria but, during the process of finding this out, you have done some real therapeutic work with the family. This work may not include a formal goal setting session with the family but the therapist should be able to record the specific aims of their work on the goal sheets.

It may be helpful to think of this as a brief intervention, consider opening a file and following up as with a full four week intervention.

Clients feelings

This first phase of the work is usually characterised by the client's feelings of hopelessness, they often want to offload their feelings of anger, depression, lack of self-worth. A workers role at this point is to accept and validate the person's feelings. Reflecting and paraphrasing. Empathising with their feelings. It is understandable that they might be angry or feeling upset considering what is happening, it is good to talk about that. Rolling with their feelings but at the same time looking for and reflecting positives, looking for exceptions when things are not so bad. Asking what makes them so strong and what strengths they have that are stopping it from getting worse. Right from this early stage people need to accept that they are doing something right, workers use many of the motivational skills and solution focussed techniques that are covered later in the book to help families begin to feel more positive.

We look in detail for strengths, positives, values and beliefs that are core to their being, put the client on a 'high' about herself and get her to dream about a better future. Using tools covered in detail later in the book, we reframe this time as a 'turning point' for the family, ask them to dream about what they could do differently, how they could take control of the situation.

Things happen very quickly at the beginning, clients usually want a lot of therapist time and energy and this can be very physically, intellectually and emotionally demanding for workers and so it is important to make sure that therapists do not take on more than one family at a time.

The next two weeks

We discuss with the family their perceptions of any immediate practical blocks to them making changes – no gas or electricity, untidy or dirty environment which challenges self-worth and lowers expectations of success. If we can help to change this, we do. We give clients models of immediate action and hopefulness. We have a small budget of £40 allocated for use with each family; this is easily accessible to the therapist and can be used immediately to dissolve some obstacles which block progress. This is not 'rescuing people', it is a tool to create hope and a belief that things can get better and create an expectation of change. Sometimes this budget will not be used and it rolls over so that an increased amount is available for other clients.

Using a card sort exercise we look in depth at people's values. What do they believe about family life? What are their hopes and dreams for their family? This exercise often creates a cognitive dissonance, a critical difference between what people believe and how they behave.

This is a powerful lever for change, the fact that they have discovered this disparity for themselves creates an uncomfortable situation where desire to change is maximised.

Using another exercise we look at the family's strengths – what is positive around and about them. This exercise focusses on the positives of the individual, family, culture, and ecology. It provides feedback that things are not *all* bad, that there are plenty of good, positive and supportive aspects around them, personal or ecological strengths. Things that can help them to cope with change.

These two processes build hope that change is possible and confidence that they are able to make those changes. They get people talking about their important beliefs. This encourages change and an acceptance of the strengths that will help to support and maintain that change. We usually find that at this point, between three and five days into the intervention, people are feeling much more positive, hopeful about the future and confident in talking honestly to us. The exercises facilitate communication and an honest exchange of beliefs, giving people the message that we actually care about what they believe and value their culture. If we value it, then they value it and are motivated to protect it. This exercise generates a long list of beliefs about family life.

By the end of the first week and into the second week we have built a rapport, the client is feeling comfortable with us, is beginning to trust us more, we continue to explore strengths and values, listening and helping people to come to terms with the present situation and we are starting to set some clear goals for the future. Together we are looking at what needs to be done to allow the family to achieve them.

Using their growing confidence and hope, we help families to create positive achievable images of the future. Using tools such as the 'Miracle Question' (which is a stock tool of Brief Solution Focussed Therapy and Neuro-Linguistic Programming) we help people to explore their preferred futures.

Into the second week things are much more stable. Building on the existing strengths and values in the family we help the family to set a number of achievable goals with clearly defined behavioural outcomes and give clear expectations of change. We negotiate goal priorities and devise, scale and score these goals in a way that enables the therapist and the family to discuss and monitor progress towards them. They provide clear indicators of success. We work on just the most important goals for each family member, no more than three each. These also are fed back to the referring social worker so that they are clear about the route our intervention is taking and so that everybody in the system is clear about what changes we are working on.

Individual goals are many and varied but they often include:

- Giving up or changing drink or drug use.
- Having better relationships with other family members.
- Creating better routines for the children.
- Managing children's behaviour.

- Having a cleaner and tidier home.

- Being calmer, more relaxed.

- Getting children to return to school.

- Help to live with depression or anxiety.

- Returning to work or education.

- Dealing with domestic violence.

- Getting fitter and healthier.

We use a 'goal attainment scaling system' which measures progress toward and beyond these goals which you will read about in Chapter 8 of this manual.

The therapist devises a plan which looks at what happens in each of the four weeks. We break down the steps towards achieving those goals and together we address these particular issues by teaching new skills, such as behaviour or anger management, time management, crisis management tools, communication skills and relaxation skills. Ideas for teaching some of these skills are included at the end of this manual.

At this stage clients begin to learn and practice new behaviours, this is usually a very hopeful stage. New ideas and behaviours will be tested and tried, perhaps workers will be modelling or coaching, stopping the action and asking about what just happened between two people and why did it happen and what it meant to each of them. At other times they may be working with clients explaining how to do something, then showing them how to do it, doing it with them then encouraging the client to do it themselves. That could be anything from diffusing an aggressive situation, negotiating a bedtime, cooking a meal or mending a bike. We find ourselves doing things that are purely about building confidence and feelings of competence in the client family and if that means helping them to hang wallpaper, we do it.

All the time the worker is looking for teachable moments, events which provide an opportunity to learn something, whilst remaining focused on the client's goals. This is why a high level of contact is so important. Workers become active participants in the daily drama of people's lives and yet because they are workers they can ask for the action to be stopped and events discussed. During that time we don't just sit there, we encourage the family to get on with whatever they were intending to do that day and we do it with them, talking about how this or that will help their preferred future to be realised or hinder it.

The final days

In the final week we are getting the client to practise, practise, practise their new routines and skills and we start to look at maintenance. What services and resources are required to enable the family to continue their progress. This might mean referrals to other agencies or arranging a maintenance meeting between the therapist, family and other key workers to plan together what needs to happen next to support the family.

The final stage is about letting go. Clients have new skills and have practised them, used them and seen that they work. Now we have to let go and allow clients to do it on their own. We tell them that we can be called to visit for a 'booster session' if things go wrong and that we will be back in four weeks anyway. We look at the family's written goals and we score them together (examples of that later).

From the beginning we are clear that this will be a brief intervention and we count down with the client, often saying things like 'we have about 12 days left so perhaps we need to get on and talk about such and such'. It comes as no surprise to clients that we are leaving and by the time we leave they are usually feeling hopeful and positive and wanting to get on with their lives.

Closing report

A report is written which focusses on the goals that have been set by the family. This includes a commentary on why those goals were chosen and the family's progress toward them. The report usually includes copies of the written feedback from paper exercises and other written material produced by/with the family. These will be about their strengths and values, an analysis of further work required to enable the family to remain together. The report, like any other recording needs to be behaviourally specific. Including only the behaviour that you have observed. You need to remember that it may be used in court proceedings. Along with the report, we send out evaluation forms to the family and the referrer, including an SAE for the family if appropriate (see Appendix).

We make sure that the report is seen by the family and agreed by them before it gets sent to the referrer. The family are given a copy for their file.

Maintenance meeting

The maintenance meeting is an innovation devised by Mandy Morgan an Option 2 therapist in a neighbouring authority. This is a meeting organised by the therapist which includes the family, the referrer and other professionals involved in the case. We will chair this meeting which will have a number of objectives.

- We will discuss the report and recommendations.

- The family will be asked what has worked well and what progress they have made.

- The professionals will be asked for their perception of what has gone well and what progress has been made.

- The worker will add any additional information and summarise the positives.

- The family is asked what they will need to do to ensure that progress will continue.

- The family is asked to identify where this support may be sought.

- The professionals are asked what they feel they can add to the maintenance plan.

- The worker summarises the maintenance plan and asks if all present agree to it.

- The worker will ensure that all the partners present receive a copy of the plan.

Follow up visits

We make contact with the family at one, three, six, and twelve months after the end of the intervention. At this time we re-scale the family's goals and record them on the statistical sheets which are in the appendix. These forms look at the goals set by the family and track the family's progress in regard to these goals for the year following our work We tend to find that most families continue to use their new coping skills and strategies and so continue to make improvements beyond their stated goal.

At follow up points we also contact the referrer and provide a written report.

Booster sessions

Our workers may work with families again for a maximum of two days. This is to respond to a crisis and reinforce some of the new coping skills. Referrals for boosters may come from family members, case managers or anybody else concerned with the family.

Conclusion

In this brief overview we have seen that the intervention is a structured one with some very clear principles and strategies. The first two weeks are a time of dealing with crisis, devising, clarifying and setting goals and devising a plan to achieve the goals. The second two weeks focus on teaching the new skills needed to achieve the goals and then practise, practise, practise of those new skills.

I have concentrated here on how we do this intervention in Cardiff. Obviously you may not be able to change the structure in which you work but you may be able to use the tools and skills that the rest of the manual contains.

This next section begins to look in detail at what skills and tools the worker needs to be able to provide a service to clients within the principles and strategies. It will be seen that appropriate communication skills underpin all of our work.

CHAPTER 3

Power and Partnership

If you don't trust the people, You make them untrustworthy.

Lao-Tzu, *Tao Te Ching*, 400 BC

It is conventional wisdom that social workers have all the power and clients have none. This causes some real problems when we start talking about working in partnership. However a moment's thought will make it obvious that clients have a much more subtle power, the power to accept or reject you as a worker. The relationship between client and worker has far more effect on outcomes than the particular intervention style. A client will choose whether they want to work with you or not based on how they perceive you. *You* may wish to hide behind your profession and be seen as instrument of the state but *they* will assess you as a human being. If they choose to reject us as workers, all we are then able to do is to react to their choices.

Written agreements

If you are going to agree to work together, some people like to have it in writing, this helps people to be clear about roles and responsibilities. Real agreements are of course negotiated, not dictated. Families know that written agreements which are not negotiated are traps for them to fall into and they will often be resistant to them. Written agreements are all too often dreamed up in social workers offices as a sort of social workers 'wish list', presented to families with the implied threat that if they do not 'comply' then their non-compliance will be seen as evidence of failure. Such threats teach people that if they want to survive intact, they must lie.

I sometimes use a written agreement. On one of my early visits to a family we will usually discuss what everybody wants to get out of this piece of work. I will be looking for an agreement that the family members want to make some changes in their lives and want to keep their family together. Most parents agree that they want their children to have a life that gives them the skills, emotional support and the protection they need for a successful and happy future. This is an agreement that we will work together for the benefit of the family, it is a real agreement because it is what they want and it is what I want, it is the basis of our work together. I often start with a standard agreement discussing it with clients and adapting it to their needs, a copy of a basic one is included in the Appendix.

Client files

When we open a new file, we create a copy file to give to the client. Each piece of written information we make is duplicated and a copy given to the client for their file. If we make daily recordings; we pass a copy on to the client, some practitioners like to make their daily recording in the form of a letter. This helps the practitioner to focus on what he is recording and his reasons for that recording. It provides an opportunity for further positive feedback to the client about what has been done and what progress has been made. Reflecting strengths and values is an opportunity to check the facts. This sharing of files makes it clear that clients are partners and that communication is open and honest.

It goes without saying that we only record directly observed facts not opinions.

Working with fear

When working with families it is wise to be acutely aware that they know that working with social services carries some very real risks for them. Risks that include being stigmatised and humiliated, risk of interference from professionals, risk of having to have lots of meetings some conflicting and interfering with their preferred functional and helpful routines, risk of their life not being their own anymore, risk that every little personal imperfection, mistake or forgotten appointment will become debated and argued over by people who they feel know nothing of them or their life, risk that life will become so complicated and stressful that they can no longer cope and ultimately the risk of losing their children. Those risks are real and inevitable for the families we work with.

Clients are often embarrassed and ashamed and only a style of communication that is motivational will be able to unlock the truth. If human beings have an embarrassing secret, the tendency is to keep it secret, or at least private. You can't expect people to look you in the eye if you are looking down on them. People may lie or mislead because they are afraid of the consequences of being honest. Often their understanding of the consequences will be inaccurate. Sometimes they are afraid because the worker is nervous or afraid and has transmitted their fear to the client in any of a number of non-verbal ways. Sometimes clients mislead because they know the social worker does not understand how the problem affects them and they fear they will jump to conclusions. Sometimes clients are having problems coping and the social worker is perceived as one of their problems rather than a real source of solutions. Sometimes, in the rarest of cases, clients lie because they are deliberately abusing their children and are frightened of being caught.

The truth is holistic

The truth consists of the whole truth, not just selected parts of it. In other words not just the bad, weak, shameful stuff but the strong, positive and hopeful stuff as well. This intervention is holistic, if you take sections of the truth out of context (positive or negative) they cease to be a real representation and become a biased personal interpretation. If you focus on the problems more than the strengths then you do not see the whole truth and when families become aware of the problem focused nature of the worker they begin to lose trust and the desire to communicate fades.

The only people who know the whole truth are the family members and so your job is to learn the whole truth from your clients, and not just to learn, but to understand what their story means to each of them. What the problems mean in the context of their strengths, personality, spirituality and beliefs. What their strengths mean in the context of their problems. You and your clients working together can make and share accurate assessments and develop intervention strategies which are useful to them as people.

Problems are unique

Childcare social workers routinely come across family members who have a whole variety of problems and difficulties; emotional problems, parenting skills, anger management, heroin addiction, alcohol misuse, domestic violence, depression, agoraphobia and any number of aspects of human behaviour and lifestyle that have an impact on parenting and child welfare. Social workers cannot be expected to be experts on every kind of problem they are likely to come across. The ability to assess how each of these impact on parenting ability is very complicated and any such problem will affect each individual differently. People go through different stages and cycles dependant upon a thousand different factors including age, position in family, relationships, emotional state, time of the year and the weather. Furthermore the age and development of the children may make them more or less resilient and so make the parents' behaviour more or less meaningful to them. Every difficulty is unique to the individual who has it and its effect on family members is different for each member at different times. It is important to take consultation with professionals in those specialist fields. Those professionals will be able to tell you the likelihood of this or that happening, the processes that most people may go through and the potentials for certain outcomes. But unless they have been working with that particular family at the same time you were, they will be unable to tell you how the problem affects them and what the outcomes are likely to be. Unless they are directly involved with the family they can only really be used for guidance, support and supervision.

It is therefore not the problem that is specialised, it is the family and it is a fundamental practitioner skill to engage and understand a client, to work in partnership with the client and to accept them as an expert on their situation. I cannot stress enough that the worker's role is to learn from the client. The family is the expert. They may not know the statistics, the relapse rates, the statistical likelihood of success, but they do know how that problem or behaviour affects their family, they do know what physical, emotional and spiritual resources they have and they know what has helped in the past and they probably have ideas about what might help in the future.

Risk

To assess risk, to plan interventions, to develop rapport and to work in partnership with clients, workers must watch and listen without coming to early judgements or conclusions. 'It is only by studying the individual family that real risks can be separated out from the imagined' (Campion, 1995). With an open state of mind, a worker can ask questions that inspire hope that things can improve and encourage clients to come up with solutions:

How will you know when it has got better?

What do you feel would make life better for your children?

The nature of social work is risk, we work with it every day, we have to be comfortable with it, negotiate it and embrace it and at the same time to focus on success. Risk exists and will not go away. Trying to make risk go away hurts people and results in intrusive and unwarranted state intervention in family life. Confidence in dealing with risk comes with clarity of assessment and understanding of the reality of the situation. Which risks are real and which are more imagined? In order to make such assessments workers and clients need to communicate.

Managing risk is difficult. As a professional you will be aware of the rare but well publicised cases when child protection has gone wrong. Our culture focusses on things going wrong, even though you will have your own successes you may be acutely aware of failure and its consequences. Even when things are looking good when working with a family it can be tempting to remind everybody of the risks and past problems. Your ability to create a balance and keep these issues on the table in a solution focussed way depends on your confidence, skill, support and your current emotional state. For example you might want to say something like:

It's great that you are doing so well Ricky, you must feel that you have made great progress since you relapsed last year

Instead of:

You might be doing well at the moment Ricky but you were here before weren't you, before it all went wrong last year.

The first statement is respectful to the changes that the client has made, it conveys trust, builds motivation, allows the client to be honest, builds hope that he can continue to improve, makes him feel worthwhile and effective and helps him to continue to improve. The second statement depresses the client, makes him think that it is not worth bothering, makes him want to keep his problems from you and makes him feel without hope, belittles him and his success and makes him mistrust you.

Some of the most worrying families to work with are those where you are concerned that risky behaviour is happening but the parents are denying it. You are not sure, you might be wrong you might be right. You don't have enough information and they are resistant to any kind of intervention. But you are getting referrals from the school and from neighbours. When you visit, the family are resistant, they are always out, they don't answer the door. They are angry and offended at your presence. The traditional way forward is to mess about for a while trying to get access, hold planning meetings and then confront this resistance head-on and enforce compliance through legal or quasi-legal interventions such as written 'agreements' and Child Protection Case Conferences. This is wasteful if brought in unnecessarily, stressful for you and doubly stressful for the family concerned. The tools in this manual will help families to open up and will help you to work effectively and quickly with those difficult cases.

You can work with risk in a solution focussed way. Focussing on solutions means accepting risk as part of human life, however instead of confronting risk head on and creating resistance in the client, we accept the risk and focus on how safety can be created or increased, along the way building trust and partnership. People will talk about risk if they feel you are working with them to create solutions. If they feel you are blaming, castigating or judging them for their risk behaviour they will clam up. Focussing on solutions does not mean that you are living in la-la land and are avoiding risk. Professional risk avoidance is usually characterised in one of two ways, either by avoiding the family, going sick, pretending that everything is alright, and avoiding the issues, or by taking too severe an action too soon. A solution focussed practitioner will not feel the need to do any of these things.

Working with families

We work with the whole family, whoever is there when we visit. We spend a great deal of time mediating between family members and helping them to negotiate. Sometimes, advocating for younger family members, often doing the counselling sessions, the card games and the paper exercises as a group. This obviously helps the family bond as they see that they are working together to better their situation. It also gives each member a greater understanding of the others. We will work quite hard to make sure that people are engaged and this can be tricky when one person engages straight away and another needs more time to get used to us.

Working with families means that sometimes we will work with the whole group and sometimes we may want to work individually with a family member, especially when they have developed different goals or if they have issues they do not want to talk about in the family group.

All of the skills which we discuss in the next sections are there to be used with individuals and with family groups.

CHAPTER 4

Communication Skills

Reinforcement is central to therapeutic efficiency . . . Expecting the client to improve plays a large part in what actually happens.

Sol Garfield, *The Practice of Brief Psychotherapy* (1989)

I always think that at the first visit of client and worker, you should have two slightly nervous people. Neither individual knows the other or what kind of agenda they have. So your task on that first visit is to make this clear as soon as possible. Before you make that visit you need to be clear in yourself why you are going there and what you intend to do when you are there. For us at Option 2 we always think that the first visit is about getting an invitation for a second visit.

It is said that 55% of all social meaning in face to face encounters comes through non verbal means. I like to start with some problem-free talk, show warmth and trust, introduce yourself to everybody there, include everybody. Shake hands if that is what people do in your culture, be yourself, ask what you should call them, use their names if they are comfortable with that. We need to wait to be invited in. When we are in we wait to be asked to sit down. We should treat the client's home and territory with respect and so we make it easier for them to communicate honestly with us.

For me, problem free talk often begins with the home. I might say something positive about a picture or ornament on the wall, how interesting their collection of trophies is. The idea is that we open conversation by talking about something positive, that is of clear importance to the individuals in the family and reflects them and myself as human beings with real private lives of our own.

This problem-free talk which is a part of Brief Solution Focussed Therapy serves to create a feeling of competence, a frame of abilities, within which the client's perception of their own incompetence can begin to change. The nature of most of the settings within which we operate means that there is a danger that we will connect with the problem of the client rather than the person of the client. The idea of problem-free talk encourages the worker to connect with the person of the client and to begin to mark in the conversation the skills, resources and strengths that the client inevitably brings, thus it is useful for the worker to ask, or at least to bear in mind, these questions:

- What is it that the client does well?

- What are the client's resources?

It is said that 55% of all social meaning in face-to-face situations comes through non verbal means.

I like to build rapport with my clients by allowing them to choose where to sit first, then if possible choosing a seating position at about 45 degrees to them. People find this position co-operative and non-threatening. In this position you can use your peripheral vision to watch their body language and respond accordingly. Moods are catching, people will learn to mirror your sense of calm and so be prepared to react to their anxious mood with a relaxed concerned one, their aggressive mood with a positive hopeful one. Physically react to their solution focussed statements by leaning in and showing an interest. Mirror their positive body language. Retain a passive, non-committal stance for their negative statements. Otherwise maintain an open position for everything.

It may sound obvious but it needs stating that it is important to smile and use good eye contact. Think about your non-verbals, be open and relaxed. Once you have established a communication, showed some respect and been given some in return, it may be time to give clear messages about why you are here, e.g.

> *I am here because I have been told that things are a little difficult for you all right now.*

Even if you know that the children had been hurt for instance, you are giving the client the opportunity to state their case, to see that you are not here to punish them but to listen to what concerns them and to help them to deal with things in a better way. Most people who hit their children do it on the spur of the moment, in anger because they do not know what else to do. Most regret it later even if they appear blustering and defensive. Remember point six of the guiding principles in Chapter 1: On the whole people are doing the best they can with what they know.

You need to gauge the clients level of concern about the issues rather than impose your own, so I find it useful to state the case in as neutral terms as I can invent at the beginning until I am able to ask about how much of a problem it is. I want to follow the clients agenda, what do they feel is important, what is to them the most pressing problem? If you feel that their level of concern is vastly lower than yours, there will be plenty of time to increase their level of concern and their intention to change using Motivational Interviewing techniques.

You need to transmit a feeling of hopefulness, without being a 'Pollyanna'. So your language should be positive, and hopeful. Make supportive statements, e.g.

> *It sounds like you have been dealing with rather a lot recently.*

You need to use behavioural descriptions of the problem and not use labels or jargon, for instance rather than talking about domestic abuse or violence you might prefer to talk about anger, frustration, jealousy and taking those feelings out on each other. It is important to 'grasp the nettle' and state the concerns but they need to be real, honest and behavioural rather than labels, labels are for identical packets of soup, not unique individuals e.g.

I am concerned that you hit Wendy.

Rather than:

I am concerned about the domestic violence.

If you have created rapport people will tell you their story. You need to reflect what they are saying, reflect the feelings they are expressing and reflect the content of what they are saying, paraphrasing, e.g.

You're feeling angry because social services say you hit your child but you don't think it was as simple as that.

Use these reflections as much as possible and try to avoid asking too many questions, you don't want a question and answer session, you want the client to feel open and free to talk and tell their story in a way that means something to them. Look for that meaning and ask for clarification if you are not sure about the meaning.

Take a guess at what the other person is feeling and thinking. Maintain eye contact and use door openers: 'Uh huh', 'Tell me more', head nodding. Parrot or paraphrase what the other has said, reflecting both feelings and content and summarising from time to time:

I don't want it to happen again.
   You don't want it to happen again.
Yes, it was awful.
   It made you feel angry.
Yes, I felt like I was going out of control.
   You don't want to get out of control.
No, I am afraid of what might happen.
   It sounds like you are afraid you might not be able to control yourself if it happens again.

You need to use this reflective listening to get the client to talk about the need to change. Obviously you need to be focussed very carefully on what the other is saying so that you can spot opportunities to do this.

You don't like to feel out of control.
   No, I can't deal with things properly and later I feel bad.
Sounds like you want to be able to deal with things better.
   Yes . . .

It is not helpful to confront the client with the need to change as that will only result in resistance, e.g.

Perhaps you need to change the way you deal with this.
   No, he needs to stop winding me up.

Observe physical cues as well as listening to words, reflect on them:

It seems to make you tense when you think about this.

It is important that you do not fall into the trap of blaming the client. Consider the following exchanges:

Why don't you go to school David?
  Because I get bullied.

and . . .

So what do you think would help you to choose to go to school?
  Well, if I wasn't bothered by bullies I might go.

The first one leads you nowhere, it focusses on David as the problem before you even know what the problem is. David feels challenged because he feels you think he is the problem, it is confrontational. The second is solution focussed and not only tells you that David feels bullied but that if he didn't feel bullied he might go to school. It leads right in to asking what he thinks could be done about the bullying. Solution focussed questions not only get you an understanding of the problem, they start to build solutions which are created and owned by the client.

Solutions devised by clients are far more likely to be used, they are more likely to be accepted by the client, they are built with the clients understanding of his beliefs and in-depth knowledge and feelings about the problem and because of this they are so are much more likely to work. If you can get clients to build their own solutions you neatly sidestep any resistance they may have to your solutions.

This style of working is a highly preferred alternative to the traditional social work route which is to gather all the information about the problem, try to come up with a solution and see if the client will go for it. This method goes straight into getting the client to define their own solution.

Pace is very important and I hope this is giving you some sense of the timing involved. You need to move along at the client's pace and avoid the common mistakes of overshooting – rushing ahead to where you want to be and undershooting or lagging behind, going over stuff that has already been covered. This can be difficult because at some point you will spot an opportunity that you feel needs following up and you will be eager to get there. But you can end up with a client who feels bored, pressurised or not listened to. By all means go back to something that you are not sure about if the client has rushed on but let them control the pace as much as possible.

You said a moment ago that things were worse in the morning, can you tell me more about that?

Be equally supportive of all family members, that means including people, accepting them, validating their feelings, empathising with them, reflecting what they say no matter what their age or gender:

So when you came back you felt out of control and you hurt Wendy. From where I stand it seems that you wish it hadn't happened.

So when the baby was screaming you just couldn't stand it any more and you left her alone, you seem to be saying that you feel bad about it and want to make sure you don't do it again.

Sometimes perhaps it doesn't feel fair when your parents tell you to come in, especially when your friends are allowed to stay out.

Sometimes you will want to check out your perceptions and encourage the client to expand on what they are saying, you may want to use phrases like:

You feel . . .
From your point of view . . .
From where you stand . . .
As you see it . . .
You think . . .
You believe . . .
You like/don't like . . .
You're . . . (identify feelings – angry, sad, overjoyed)
I'm picking up that you . . .
You want . . .

Sometimes you are not so sure what the client means, you are not picking it up or are feeling a little confused, having difficulty perceiving clearly. You could use phrases like:

Could it be that . . .
I wonder if . . .
I'm not sure if I'm wrong, but . . .
Is it possible that . . .
From where I stand, you . . .
You appear to be feeling . . .
Perhaps you are feeling . . .
I somehow sense that maybe you feel . . .
Is there any chance that you . . .
Maybe you feel . . .
You seem to be saying that . . .

The idea is not to ask direct questions but to reflect what you are receiving and see if you are right:

You seem to be saying that you don't know what they meant.

If you are right the client may say something like:

That's right, I feel confused about it because that is not what they were saying yesterday . . .

If you are wrong the client will tell you:

*No, I mean I was angry because **he** said that . . .*

In both cases they will naturally expand on what they are telling you.

When people go quiet, let them. Often during this time they are thinking about what they mean and how they can express it in a way that will be easily understood. People think in different ways, some are obviously thinking, making facial expressions, others may just appear blank while the answer filters down from their subconscious. Give them time to think. At other times people go quiet because they do not understand what you are asking of them, again they need time to process this, then again some people sometimes just drift off into a reverie of their own. Occasionally you may want to make a short interjection to test this hypothesis:

Does that make sense?
Is that familiar to you?

Throughout this communication it is your responsibility to model calmness, verbally and non-verbally. Do not make commands or suggestions but if you feel compelled to show people an alternative way you may use self-disclosure very occasionally, for example:

What sometimes works for me is if I speak quietly and clearly instead of shouting.

Working together

Very often you will find yourself in a sitting room or kitchen with parents, children and grandparents. They are all your clients. I like to think of the family as a single entity. Often my work is to get the different parts of that entity to work together harmoniously. Using reflective listening skills you will be able to help each party to express themselves and find the middle ground in negotiating their way through situations that have been problematical. It can often be very enlightening for a parent to hear their child's view of the world and of their parenting. Children can sometimes gain an understanding of their parents' fears and reasons for behaving the way they do. This sets the scene for developing trust and compromise between parties. It can sometimes be helpful to ask some family members to be observers for a short period so that another family member has the space to express themselves.

Negotiating resolutions

It is often important to teach clients how to negotiate with other family members without freezing the show with statements like 'take it or leave it', 'This is the way it is, like it or lump it', when people are belligerent like this, it prevents further negotiation, it makes people react negatively and decide that the relationship is not worth having. If parents want to have a relationship with their children as they get older, more mature and own more personal power and confidence, they must learn how to negotiate. As children change and develop, so must parents.

It is your job to uncover the real needs and interests of each party, these may be very different from the stated interests so you need to turn off your inner dialogue, watch the non-verbals and really listen. This is a process that can take some time and energy.

Negotiating is about finding the middle way. The process has three stages.

Phase one is about sharing information. Ask each member what difference they would notice if they resolved the problem. Analysis and understanding of the issues and establishing rapport, creating an environment of partnership where each party has the same harmonious goal with something to gain and something to offer. Focus on being partners in solving the problem, not opponents. You are looking for a win/win situation where nobody loses too much and everybody gains something. You need to look at each party's best case scenario and worst case scenario; the area between the two ends of the scale is the bargaining area. You need to assume that the solution is somewhere in the middle and create that expectation in the two parties.

Phase two is about making opening offers. Being creative and brainstorming potential solutions. It is important to focus on the issue rather than personalities by looking at what is fair for both parties. It can help to divide the issue into parts and address a less difficult part when you get stuck. Invite trading, ('if you will, then I will'). Let each person take turns, make a move and see what the response is, co-operate in finding a solution. Look at what concessions each party is willing to make in order to get closer to a life they would like.

Phase three is about agreement, writing it down if appropriate. Emotional closure, helping everybody to feel a winner and looking at how life could be now a resolution has been agreed. Talk about how finding solutions is about development and growth. You can always contract with each party to a trial period and a review date.

The basic principles are to focus on needs rather than personalities. See the section on 'I' messages later in the book. Emphasise common ground, reframe personal attacks as attacks on the issue and unhelpful behaviours as tactics. It is important to maintain the relationship and to understand that everything is negotiable. People who are very good at negotiating often appear to be really enjoying themselves. Understand that what is fair and acceptable is not a clear point, it is a range of acceptable positions. Remind parties that generosity begets generosity. Make it possible for people to change their position without appearing to back down or feel humiliated. Praise people for being willing to move and accept the other's view. You may have to let some attacks and ultimatums from less skilled negotiators pass by. Every now and then, summarise how far you have got and review common ground and agreements already reached. If the meeting gets heated then you can call for a break to review progress made so far.

Joining with clients

1 Can I be perceived by the other person as trustworthy, as dependable or consistent in some deep sense?

2 Can I express myself enough as a person that the one I'm helping will know the real me?

3 Can I let myself experience positive attitudes toward this other person – attitudes of warmth, caring, liking, interest, respect?

4 Am I secure enough with myself to permit him to be himself? Can I give him the freedom to be who he is, or do I feel that he should follow my advice, etc?

5 Can I let myself enter fully into the world of her feelings and personal meanings and see these as she does? Can I step into her private world so completely that I lose all desire to evaluate or judge it?

6 Can I be accepting of each facet of this other person, which he represents to me? Can I receive him as he is? Can I communicate this attitude?

7 Can I act with sufficient sensitivity in the relationship that my behaviour will not be perceived as a threat? If I can free her as completely as possible from external threat, then she can begin to experience and to deal with the internal feelings and conflicts, which she finds threatening within herself.

8 Can I free him from the threat of external evaluation? The meaning and value of his experience is something, which is up to him, and no amount of external judgement can alter this.

9 Can I meet this other individual as a person who is in process of becoming, or will I be bound by her past and by my past?

Traps to avoid as a helper

The question-answer trap

Use open-ended questions and reflective listening. Clients should not be able to respond with a simple yes or no.

The confrontational/denial trap

Use reflective listening to get people to talk about the need to change.

The expert trap

Give the person the opportunity to think about and solve the uncertainty about change for themselves.

The labelling trap

Instead of labelling behaviour as 'Domestic Violence' say: 'It doesn't matter what we call a problem, what matters is how hitting each other harms both of you and what, if anything, you want to do about it'.

The early solution trap

You may know there is a particular problem and you may feel strongly that they need to change right now, but you need to start with clients' concerns. Let them talk to you about what they see is the problem. You may learn something.

The blaming trap

Help is not about who is at fault, but rather about what's troubling you and what you want to do about it.

This is an approach that allows people to speak about their concerns rather than resisting and denying the concerns raised by a worker. In this communication style you do not confront resistance, you roll with it, you will read more about this in the section on Motivational Interviewing. These communication skills are the basic tools of anybody whose job it is to help others. After a brief discussion of Cognitive Dissonance there follows some more advanced applications of these skills.

Cognitive dissonance

Much of how we communicate with families involves creating and building a cognitive dissonance. This is a difference between how the individual behaves, and what their values are about how they should behave. It is easier for people to change their behaviour than their beliefs so if their behaviour does not fit with their beliefs, there is a subconscious push towards changing behaviour in a way which fits in with beliefs. Griffin (1997) describes it as a 'distressing mental state . . .'

This is a theory devised by psychologist Leon Festinger from Stanford University in 1957. Festinger claimed that people avoid information that is likely to increase dissonance. He believed that dissonance could be heightened by the importance of the issue, the longer it takes to make a decision and how hard it is to reverse the decision once it has been made. These factors make the person wonder if they have made the right choice and after they have made a tough choice they are motivated to seek support and reassurance for their decision. For us as workers therefore our role is to accept and acknowledge the persons history, look at the consequences of making different choices and to reassure the client after they have made a choice.

Much of our work creates the opportunity to plant a 'seed' that will irritate the client into making a change. People avoid information that creates a dissonance between what they believe and how they act. We present them with their own personal beliefs that, because of their aspirational nature, often conflict with how they act in a day-to-day way. We plant the seed of change. People are less likely to want to change good self belief, for less positive beliefs about themselves.

When a parent tells us that he is a caring parent who strives to be calm at all times, it is likely to make him try to be more caring and calm. He is more likely to notice when he is being uncaring and become stressed because that is not who he believes he really is. This is the same process used by people who use visualisation and positive thinking when they look in a mirror each morning and make an affirmation such as: 'I am a beautiful and joyful manifestation of the energy of the universe'. (Try it . . .). Saying it makes it more true.

Cognitive dissonance in motivational interviewing and brief solution focussed therapy are discussed in the next two chapters. These are two intervention styles which are both highly motivational and solution focussed, but I felt it was worth looking at these two styles separately because although they have much in common they do require different skills.

Constructive feedback

Constructive feedback is a vital part of this intervention. Many of the exercises that we will talk about later on rely on the power of constructive feedback for their efficacy. Throughout each session it is very important to notice anything which might contribute to the client reaching his or her goal. This might be reported behaviour, attitude during the session, responses of other people, evidence of survival, determination and perseverance. The more the client is told of what is noticed the more he or she is likely to continue with this behaviour.

> *So you want to take control of this situation and make life better.*
> *You seem very positive about that . . .*
> *I notice that you are both nodding your heads and agreeing with each other, I guess you are a strong couple.*

All sessions end with a summary of feedback. It is important to feedback about constructive behaviour. That may include client's goals to do something about problem areas:

> *You have told me about a lot of strengths today, the fact that you are a strong couple, you care deeply about each other and about your children. You have been able to talk about successes in the past in dealing with problems with communication and you have said some very positive things about how you want to find new ways of dealing with emotions that lead to losing your temper. You seem to be very hopeful about the future . . .*

This feedback can be reinforced by the worker giving copies of their daily recording to the client and copies of feedback from exercises that we will discuss later.

CHAPTER 5

Motivational Interviewing

The client is the one who controls the possibility of improvement. The therapist cannot step out of the boundaries of the client's expectations and tolerance. The therapist has to be seen to be a plausible healer.

The therapist has to have at least a minimum belief in the motivation, co-operation, competence and resources of the (client).

Sol Garfield, *The Practice of Brief Psychotherapy* (1989)

Motivational Interviewing (MI) was developed by Bill Miller and Steve Rollnick in the UK. It has a theoretical background in the principles of Egan (problem solving) and Rogers' (accurate empathy and behavioural psychology (by changing what you do, you change what you think), see Miller and Rollnick (1991).

Social workers often meet with resistance from service users. MI uses the persons own values and goals to bring about change. It does this by creating a discrepancy between people's current behaviour and what they want to achieve. MI has a very powerful ability to motivate people to change and to overcome their objections to change.

The strategies of Motivational Interviewing are completely non-confrontational, persuasive and supportive. The style is empathic with the emphasis on listening, accepting and understanding the client without judging or necessarily agreeing or disagreeing with what is being said. This is a communication style which allows individuals to address problems which they might otherwise avoid or deny having. It is particularly powerful technique for helping families to get 'unstuck'.

It is a fundamental belief that each person has the ability to change. The workers role is to increase the client's motivation and to help the client to explore and voice the reasons for change. We want clients to present the arguments for change, voice their own reasons and to make their own self motivational statements.

Resistance

The concept of resistance is a very important one when working with families who have problems. Resistance takes many forms:

Argument

The person contests the accuracy, expertise, or integrity of the helper:

- Challenging – the person directly challenges the accuracy of what the helper has said.

- Discounting – the person questions the helper's personal authority and expertise.

- Hostility – the person expresses direct hostility toward the helper.

Interruption

The person breaks in and interrupts the helper in a defensive manner:

- Talking Over – the person speaks while the helper is still talking, without waiting for an appropriate pause or silence.

- Cutting Off – the person breaks in with words obviously intended to cut the helper off. 'Now wait a minute – I've heard about enough'.

Denial

The person expresses an unwillingness to recognise problems, co-operate, accept responsibility, or take advice (not a character flaw):

- Blaming – the person blames other people for problems.

- Disagreeing – the person disagrees with a suggestion that the helper has made, offering no constructive alternative. (This includes the familiar 'Yes, but . . .')

- Excusing – the person makes excuses for their behaviour.

- Not me – the person claims that they are not in danger.

- Minimising – the person suggests that the helper is exaggerating risks or dangers, and that it 'really isn't so bad'.

- Pessimism – the person makes general statements about self or others that are pessimistic, defeatist, or negative in tone.

- Reluctance – the person expresses reservations and reluctance about the information or advice given.

- Unwilling to change – the person expresses a lack of desire or an unwillingness to change, or an intention not to change.

Ignoring

The person shows evidence of not following/ ignoring the helper:

- Inattention – The person's response indicates that they have not been following or attending to the helper.

- Non-answer – in answering a helper's query, the person gives a response that is not an answer to the question or they give no audible or a non-verbal reply to a helper's query.

■ Sidetracking – the person changes the direction of the conversation that the helper has been pursuing.

■ Not doing what they said they would do.

Rolling with resistance

Resistance is a signal for the worker to change strategies. Digging your heels in, taking a stand and confronting a problem head on is counter productive, confrontation creates resistance and so the aim is to be fluid, to change strategies, to roll and flow. Momentum can be used to good advantage and perceptions can be shifted. Here are some examples of rolling with resistance:

Listening

Respond to resistance with non-resistance:

> *I'm not the one with the problem. If I drink too much, it's just because my kids are always nagging me.* (Denying-blaming)
> > *It seems to you that the real reason you drink so much has to do with problems with how the kids behave.*

Shifting focus

Shift the person's attention away from what seems to be a stumbling block:

> *I know that what you want is for me to be the perfect mum and never hit my kids, but I'm not going to do that.*
> > *I don't want us to get stuck on that one thing. I'm more interested in how you see things about . . . (then change the topic).*

Agreement with a twist

Offer initial agreement but with a slight twist:

> *Why are you and my parents so stuck on my drinking? What about all their problems? You'd drink too, if your family was nagging you all the time and locking the doors to keep you out.*
> > *You've got a good point there, and that's important. There is a bigger picture here and maybe I haven't been paying enough attention to that. It's not as simple as one person's drinking; I agree with you that we shouldn't be trying to place blame here. Problems like these do involve the whole family. I think you're absolutely right.'*

It's up to you

Phenomenon of reactance: when people think that their freedom of choice is being threatened, they tend to react by asserting their liberty. It is advised to *not* use this response to resistance when the harm is so high that the helper cannot risk the parent making a choice to continue that harm.

I'll show you; nobody tells me what to do!

Assure the person that in the end, it is they who determine what happens, even if the harmful behaviour continues resulting in the removal of the children. Let them know that you want to help keep the family together, and say things like:

What you do with this information is completely up to you.
Nobody can change your behaviour for you. It's really your decision.
I can't decide for you, and I couldn't change you, even if wanted to. You're a free person, it's up to you.
If you decided that you don't want to change, then you won't. If you want to change, you can. It's your choice, I can only help you make the best choice, or take other action if the kids remain at risk.

A new way to look at it

Reframe the information that the person is offering. The approach acknowledges the validity of the person's raw observations, but offers a new meaning or interpretation for them:

My kids quit their fighting when I threaten them, so it works.
That's an interesting situation actually. It seems that some kids do quit the immediate behaviour, but don't understand how to keep doing that. Instead, they just fight again, until you threaten them again, and so on. Have you ever noticed that?

Self-motivational statements

In one sense Motivational Interviewing is the opposite of a confrontation-of denial approach in which the helper promotes the problem-change position.

In Motivational Interviewing it is the client who presents the arguments for change. The workers goal is to have the client take the 'opposite' side of the argument.

We want the client to do several things, firstly we want them to recognise that there is a problem, then we want them to understand that the problem concerns them, then we want them to voice reasons for and intention to change and then we want them to feel optimistic that they can do so. This is a process moving from one stage to another, sometimes going backward and forward between two stages for a while but moving onward to the point where the client recognises the problem, sees their part in it, wants to change and feels optimistic that they can change.

Sample questions for eliciting self-motivational statements

Problem recognition

What difficulties have you had regarding disciplining the children?
In what ways do you think you or other people have been harmed?
In what ways has this been a problem for you?
How has your use of spanking stopped the children from doing what you don't want them to do?
What might happen if you and I don't work together on this situation?

Concerns

What is there about your moods that you or other people might see as reasons for concern?
What worries you about your child's lack of development?
What can you imagine happening to her if this doesn't change?
How do you feel about the crying when you hit the children?
In what ways does this concern you?
What do you think will happen if you don't make a change?

Intention to change

The fact that we're here together indicates that at least a part of you thinks it's time to do something. Tell me about that.
What reasons do you see for changing how you discipline your children?
What makes you think that you may need to make a change in your drug use?
If you were 100 per cent successful and things worked out exactly as you would like, what would be different?
What things make you think you should keep on drinking the way you have been? And what about the other side? What makes you think it's time for change?
As we've talked about, leaving your children alone is not okay. What are you thinking about changing regarding that?
What would be the advantages of making a change?
I can see that you're feeling stuck at the moment. What's going to have to change so your kids can stay here with you?

Optimism

What makes you think that if you did decide to make a change you could do it?
How will your relationship with your children improve when you do this?
What's the best outcome for your family to result when you stop hitting each other?

What encourages you that you can change if you want to?
What do you think would work for you, if you decided to change?

If you provide the right environment clients will clearly state that they can see problems, if you use the kinds of questions we have been looking at, you may be able to elicit statements like these from the person you are helping.

Sample client self-motivational statements

Problem recognition

The person expresses recognition of problems, negative consequences, or difficulties, and more generally of a need for change:

> *I guess there's more of a problem here than I thought.*
> *I never realised how much my drinking resulted in the kids getting left alone and getting hurt.*
> *This is serious!*
> *I don't think my problem with depression is dangerous or anything, but I never thought about how it affects others.*
> *Maybe I have been taking foolish risks, leaving the kids alone while I go out.*
> *I can see that in the long run, my hitting the kids is going to cause lots of problems.*

Concern

The person voices or otherwise evidences personal concern for their own condition, health, family etc.

> *I'm really worried about this.*
> *How could this happen to me? I can't believe it! I never wanted to hurt them.*
> *I feel pretty hopeless about my future if I keep getting more and more involved in hurting myself and others.*

(non-verbally through the person's facial expressions, sighs, tears, or gestures.)

Intention to change

The person indicates commitment or decision to change; direct or implicit intention to change (taking initial step):

> *I think it's time for me to think about other ways to discipline them.*
> *I've got to do something about this.*
> *This isn't how I want to be. What can I do?*
> *I don't know how I'm going to do it, but I've got to make a change.*
> *How do people quit a habit like this?*

Optimism

The person indicates hopefulness or optimism about his or her ability to change (self-efficacy):

> *I think I can do it.*
> *My kids and I won't fight so much if I quit smoking crack, so I'll be a better mum.*
> *Now that I've decided, I'm sure I can change.*
> *When I was doing better, my kids and I had a great time together. That can happen again.*
> *I'm going to overcome this problem.*

MI is a gentle strategy which uses the clients own values and beliefs to motivate people to change. The worker explores the discrepancy between how a client is behaving and what they believe, creating a cognitive dissonance within the client. This acts as an irritant and a motivator for change. There will be more about this later.

Ambivalence

Ambivalence is a state of mind where a person has conflicting feelings about something. 'I want to because . . . but I don't want to because . . .' One reason why brief interventions work so well is that they may help clients to get 'unstuck' from their ambivalence (Miller and Rollnick, 1991). Using the clients understanding of their problems we openly explore the consequences of change and no-change. One tool that I like to use to discuss and resolve ambivalence is a 'decisional balance'. With the client I like to draw a chart that looks like this:

Good things about change	Bad things about change
Good things about staying the same	Bad things about staying the same

I ask clients to tell me the good things and bad things about change and staying the same. It is important to acknowledge that there are good things about the problem. Often used with clients who have drink or drug problems. A client will quickly come up with a whole list of answers for each box, pretty soon it will be seen that the boxes do not actually balance and the reasons for change literally outweigh the reasons to stay the same. Some clients will be seen to really struggle to create reasons to stay the same and this is an excellent opportunity for the worker to reflect the fact that they are struggling.

Stages of change

From Prochaska and Di Clemente in Miller and Rollnick (1991)

Change is a process rather than an event. It is characterised by a series of stages. In attempting to change, a person typically cycles through these stages of change. Often people experience the whole cycle a number of times before finally changing the behaviour and leaving the cycle, sometimes this is described as a spiral. People entering at a lower level and going through similar stages a number of times before they leave.

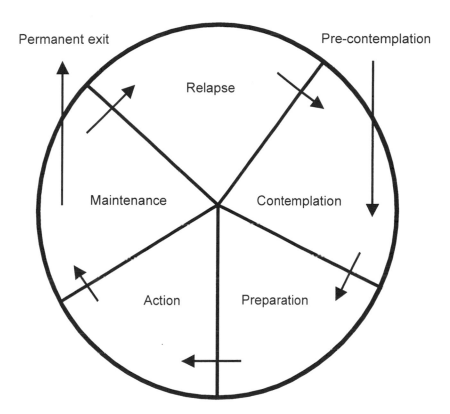

The charts on the following pages look at what is going on in each of the stages and what workers can be doing about it.

Pre-contemplation

Description	Client indicators	Worker tasks and skills
This is the entry point of a person into the change process. The individual has not even considered the prospect of change. The individual is unlikely to perceive a problem. At this stage, a person is not likely to respond positively to a worker being confrontational or demanding change.	▪ Total resistance to doing anything ▪ No willingness to meet, talk to the worker, or get assessed ▪ Angry at any indication from another that there is a problem ▪ Blaming others ▪ 'Everything is OK' statements ▪ Willingness to work on the issues of concern. ▪ Refuse to let the worker in and work with them ▪ Lack of awareness ▪ Believes there is no connection between their behaviour and the problems	▪ Engage the client ▪ Diffuse the crises ▪ Assess safety concerns ▪ Show empathy and caring ▪ Provide needed services in other areas ▪ Assess strengths and values ▪ Build a relationship ▪ Affirm the individual's strengths and capacity to the point he or she feels competent to change if he or she wishes to do so ▪ Provide information and feedback on the possible risks of client behaviour to raise the awareness of the problem and the possibility of change ▪ Listen for windows of opportunity where the client talks about problems, concerns and need to change ▪ Provide specific information the person requests

Contemplation

Description	Client indicators	Worker tasks and skills
Once the person has some awareness of the problem, then the person enters the stage called Contemplation. It is a state of ambivalence, where the individual both considers change and rejects it. If allowed to	▪ Saying one thing, doing another ▪ Rationalisations ▪ Minimising ▪ Their anxiety is rising ▪ Trying some things which are not working ▪ Both talking about change, and arguing against it	▪ Help tip the balance to favour change ▪ Evoke reasons to change and risks of not changing ▪ Continue to strengthen the client's self-efficacy ▪ Strategic use of open-ended questions, affirmations, reflective listening, summarising

just talk about it, the person goes back and forth about the need to change, and there being no justification for change.

- Have the client give voice to problem, concern, and intention to change
- Client self-assessment of values, strengths and needs.

Preparation

Description	Client indicators	Worker tasks and skills
The client is ready to change. This is a window of opportunity when the client has resolved the ambivalence enough to look at making change.	■ Admitting the need to change ■ Accepting negatives of their use behaviour ■ Asking for help ■ Saying things like 'I'm ready' ■ Starting to look at alternatives	■ Facilitate the client developing a vision for their future ■ Provide information on available options ■ Explore all available options, and the benefits and consequences of each ■ Help client develop a plan ■ Help client choose strategies to start with, resources needed, and potential barriers to the plan

Action

Description	Client indicators	Worker tasks and skills
The client engages in particular actions intended to bring about change.	■ They are starting to work to a plan ■ They are making changes in their usual behaviour ■ They are asking for your help, or using your help to make their plan more successful	■ Introduce and practice coping strategies to avoid, change, replace, or change a client's reactions to triggers ■ Suggest methods, provide support in trying them out, and help evaluate the effectiveness of those methods ■ Keep steps small and incremental ■ Teach skills to client ■ Access resources for the client to use

Action (continued)

- Reward small steps of progress
- Assess success
- Make needed changes in the plan as the client continues

Maintenance

Description	Client Indicators	Worker tasks and skills
The client identifies and implements strategies to maintain progress, and to reduce the likelihood of slips or a full relapse into old behaviours.	▪ They are making the long-term life changes needed to 'actualise' the changes made in action ▪ They focus on a better lifestyle	▪ Assist the client to sustain changes accomplished by the previous actions ▪ Help client to develop the skills and self-efficacy to build a new life ▪ Build relapse roadmaps ▪ Prepare crisis plans for when a relapse might happen ▪ Review warning signs of possible slip or relapse ▪ Help client connect to a support system for this improved lifestyle

Relapse

Description	Client Indicators	Worker Tasks and Skills
The client has a slip. At times, the client may slip and not regard it as serious enough to be concerned, yet someone may be at risk, so the worker needs to help the client look holistically.	▪ Client reverts to behaviours they are trying to stop ▪ Client begins to see this as failure	▪ Assist the client in processing the emotions resulting from the slip ▪ Help the client to understand what happened leading up to the slip ▪ Help the client to process the experience and use the slip as a learning experience ▪ Review the plan and commitment to continue ▪ Adjust plan as needed and implement it

CHAPTER 6

Solution Focussed Brief Therapy

What you focus on grows.

Patanjali (the father of Yoga), 300 BC

Solution Focussed Brief Therapy (SFBT) was originally developed by Steve de Shazer and the team at the Brief Family Therapy Centre in Milwaukee in the1980s. Its sources of inspiration include the Brief Therapy Centre at the Mental Research Institute (MRI) in Palo Alto, California, and the work of Milton Erickson in Phoenix, Arizona. The MRI's interest in interactional features of problems and Erickson's ability to 'utilise' whatever the client brings to therapy led de Shazer to a therapeutic milestone. With his notion of *exceptions* he and his team began to take familiar concepts and reshape them into a radically different sort of therapy.

This is a communication style which has some similarities with Motivational Interviewing, the main difference being that the worker's role is not to talk about the problems, but to focus on exceptions to when the problem occurs:

The exceptions to the problem are the seeds of the solution.

(Steve De Shazer)

Clients may have struggled for many years and may now be faced with one of the greatest of all threats – losing their children. The situation often feels hopeless. Solution focussed thinking however suggests that losing their children is only one prediction in a future which has yet to be determined.

By concentrating on what people are doing wrong we may be perhaps inadvertently increasing the likelihood of such a negative outcome. As workers we have to acknowledge the current problems but sensitively move the discussion on to exception finding, those exception times will show us the unique strengths and resources that people have.

The more people hear themselves describing the times when they have managed well the more likely they are to take responsibility for their successes and do more of the positive behaviours. In this way they begin to take steps towards their preferred futures.

Change will come about through the client's successful use of their skills, strengths and resources. It is useful to get in touch with those things as soon as possible. When our clients know that we recognise that they are more than the sum of their problems, they seem to feel free to talk more freely about what it is that they wish to change.

Pre-session change

It is always worthwhile asking about whatever changes the client is able to identify that have taken place before the first face-to-face meeting. Often, accepting help is the first step in a new approach to problem-solving and this first step can lead spontaneously to others (just as sometimes a toothache clears up before the dentist can treat it.) The particular usefulness of pre-session change for the worker is that the client can take total responsibility for it, and the meaning of such change is therefore particularly enhancing:

> *What differences have you noticed between when you agreed to see me and today?*
> *What differences have there been between the day that I rang and today?*

Goal setting

For any therapy to be brief and empowering it is important that the goals of that work be clear, after all, 'If you don't know where you are going you will probably end up somewhere else' (anon). If the goals are not clear then the client will not know when the goals are attained and will not know when progress is being made toward those goals. Later in the manual there are examples of how we describe and record goals in a written way that is measurable and useful to client and agency. Solution focussed workers have developed a number of questions which have been useful in achieving the sort of clear, concrete, observable goals that seem to be most useful in facilitating change:

> *How will you know at the end of the session that it was worthwhile seeing me?*
> *How will your social worker know that it is OK to stop worrying?*
> *After you have gone to bed tonight, a miracle happens and the problems that brought you here today are resolved. But you are asleep, so you will not know that the miracle has happened. When you wake up tomorrow morning what will be different that will tell you? What will you see yourself doing differently that will tell you that the miracle has happened?*

This last question, the Miracle Question as it has become known, can be used in a number of ways: as a 'guided fantasy' about a perfect future or as a detailed description of an ordinary day but one without the problem. Its importance is as a vehicle for eliciting from the client in as much detail as possible what his or her life will be like after the problem has gone. The clearer this picture is drawn the more likely it is to happen.

Exception finding

With virtually every problem our clients experience there are exceptions. These exceptions often begin the process of disintegration of the problem. In terms of the client's view of him or herself there is a great difference between the idea that the problem always happens and the client has no power and no control, and the idea that the problem might only happen in specific circumstances or that at times it does not happen, or that at times the client can refuse the problem behaviour and be in charge.

Once families are beginning to realise that they are responsible for the exception times – and we can blame them for their successes, we can start to find out about the strengths which create those exceptions and explore a view of the person's life that is a very different to the story that is normally repeated, but just as accurate.

Questions which help to elicit exceptions may be:

> *Tell me about the times it doesn't happen?*
> *Tell me about the times that it happens less?*
> *When are the times that it bothers you least?*
> *When do you resist the urge to? . . .*
> *What was life like before?*

In order to develop a prescription for action once exceptions have been elicited the worker and client need to figure out a further step:

> *What are you doing differently and what are others doing that is different at those (exception) times?*

In all of these questions, the more detailed the descriptions the more useful they are likely to be to the client. The client needs to be guided to go into deep detail about these scenarios, talking about times of day, colours, smells, who was there, what happened before and after and how they felt. They need to develop an understanding of them, an acceptance of them as real and valuable events and as part of who they are as people. Very often people have very negative self images and we need to help them to see that it is not bad all of the time and that in fact they are more balanced than they think.

Scaling

Scaling questions help families' to plot their next small steps using their unique strengths and resources. They move away from the problem behaviours and towards a more acceptable future where the children can remain safely within the family. There will inevitably be set backs and lapses but a continued interest in what's still working in spite of these will motivate and move things in a positive direction.

Measuring change can be a key tool in encouraging more change in the client. The more that the client has a sense of change, the more that they know that they are moving forward. And of course the more that the client has a sense of moving forward, the more that they will become aware of their ability to take control of their life in the face of the symptoms and the more likely that they will do more. Scaling questions are perhaps the most flexible of the solution focussed worker's tools. They can be used in a multitude of ways:

> *On a scale of one to ten, with one being the worst that things have been in your life and ten representing how you want things to be, where are you today?*

Few clients answer this question with one. This immediately gives the worker the opportunity to ask:

> *So what is it that you are doing that means that you are at . . . and not at one?*

This question opens the way to identifying both pre-session change and exceptions. However in addition, for many clients, it represents a clear and approachable way of asking about goals:

> *How will your life look when you're at ten?*

In addition it is a useful way of identifying the 'first small sign' that will show the client that change is taking place:

So if you are on three, tell me what you will be doing differently when you are on four?

> *Scaling questions can be used in follow-up sessions to trace, explore and measure change:*
>
> *Where are you today?*
> *So what have you done to move up two points since Friday?*
> *What are you doing differently?*

Scaling questions can be used to elicit how much the client wants change and their confidence in change happening:

> *On a scale of one to ten how would you rate your desire for change?*
> *What would be happening when it is one point higher?*
> *On a similar scale how do you rate your confidence that the problem will be resolved?*

Scaling questions can also be used to break complex situations down into manageable parts:

> *When your relationship with your partner moves up one point what difference do you think this will make to your child's 'behaviour scale'?*

Reluctant clients

Reluctant clients are people who come to see us when they would rather be doing something else. They have come because someone else thinks it is a good idea or because we are a route to a resource. The key to co-operation in these circumstances is to elicit and take seriously the client's goals. Maintaining a constant interest in what the client wants to achieve, provided it is not illegal or puts themselves or others at serious risk, is one of the surest routes to co-operation which in turn provides a foundation for negotiation. Taking the client's goals seriously does not diminish the importance of agency goals (e.g. child protection, school attendance, law-abiding behaviour or mental health) but rather encourages collaboration and the negotiation of mutually acceptable means. Clients often say their goal is to get professionals out of their lives. Professionals often say their job is to put themselves out of business!

Whenever a client appears 'resistant' to what we are doing we try to change and roll with that resistance and so demonstrate to the client our wish to co-operate with them.

Steve De Shazer once commented that 'Solution Focussed Brief Therapy is simple and very, very hard to do'. Challenges will always be presented and things never follow a clear plan and chronology as is sometimes presented in the key texts.

Fundamentally however if we are to achieve success for families it is about highlighting 'Strengths' and 'Resources'. People change by utilising their own unique abilities **not** by examining problems. Solution Focussed Brief Therapy gives us the questioning framework to find those strengths and resources and a structure to encourage people to best utilise them. At best miracles can happen, at worst we don't do any further harm.

The miracle question

Without playing with fantasy no creative work has ever yet to come.

Carl Jung

If one advances in the direction of his dreams . . . he will meet with success.

Henry David Thoreau

The Miracle Question is a standard tool of Solution Focussed Brief Therapy (SFBT) and Neuro-Linguistic Programming (NLP). It is used to help clients generate descriptions of their dreams and visions for the future. Through this question they dare to dream about a better life for themselves, to remember hopes and aspirations they once had but somehow gave up on. The question generates a feeling of hope, planning for the future and often a vast number of treatment solutions. There are many ways to phrase the question, here is a version as recommended by Insoo Kim Berg, a pioneer in the field of SFBT:

Now I am going to ask you a rather strange question. After we finish talking today, obviously I am going to go back to my office and you will do your routine – whatever you need to do the rest of the day, such as feeding the children, looking over their homework, watching TV or whatever. And of course later it will be time to go to bed. And when all of your family members are sleeping and the house is very quiet, in the middle of the night, a miracle happens – and the miracle is that the problems you might have with your family, or other people think that you have, all the problems you face are solved . . . Poof! Gone! But because all this happens when you and your family are asleep, nobody knows that the problems are all solved . . . So when you are slowly coming out of your sleep, what differences will you notice that will make you wonder if there was a miracle overnight and the problem is solved?

Often clients will respond by saying 'I don't know'. Greet this with silence for a moment to allow the idea to sink in. Soon they will begin to formulate an answer. Therapists are often concerned that clients will respond with an unrealistic answer 'Win the Lottery' or 'Have a nice big house in the country with horses' or 'I would have a good man who will look after me and the children'. You may be surprised that clients will often respond with small, concrete answers like 'I would get up and get dressed', 'The children would come in and smile at me', 'I wouldn't need my drugs'.

Your next task is to weave the client's vision into a solution that they can begin to implement. For example:

I wouldn't need my drugs.
 You wouldn't need your drugs, how would you know?
I would feel strong and confident.
 You would feel strong and confident because you didn't need your drugs.
Yes, I would be happier.
 How would your children know you were feeling like this?
I would smile and talk to them instead of snapping at them.
 How do you think they would feel?
Happier, calmer.
 What else would be different on this day?
The house would be tidier.
 Tell me more.
It would be clean and things would be put away.
 Who put them away?
I did.
 You put things away and tidied up. What helped you to do that?
Having more energy.
 So on this day you wake up with more energy, happier, calmer, the children are happy, our place is clean and tidy, you don't need your drugs.
That's right.
 How would you know they were feeling happier?
They wouldn't be so aggressive, they would want to spend time with me and they would be easier to get to school.
 What else would be different?

We are beginning to generate a positive vision of the future that hangs on the client formulating and implementing a goal to change her drug use. We have woven this into a network that has an impact on her environment, her children's behaviour and her relationship with them.

We could now begin to ask about exceptions, times in the past when things have been going well:

> *Tell me about a time when you didn't need your drugs.*
> *When I came out of rehab, I was clean for five months.*
> *What helped you to be successful for five months?*

If we felt the client was ready to talk about setting goals we could press on and ask a scaling question:

> *On a scale of 0 to 10 with 0 being the worst that things have been and 10 being*
> *how you want things to be, where are you now?*
> *I suppose I am about a four.*
> *So how would you know that you were at a five?*
> *I suppose that I will be doing something about the drugs.*

You can see in this dialogue the client has moved from talking about their need for drugs to talking about doing something about their need. They have also connected their drug taking to the children's behaviour and being the best parent they can be. The worker can go on and reinforce the clients talk about dealing with the drugs by asking about for example: how will things be different and what will other people notice about you?

With an imaginative, visually oriented client you can have the client go into great detail in their visualisation, be gentle, take your time. Ask about colours, smells, sounds, who is where? What would everybody else in the family be doing? Ask about the furniture, the garden, the colour of the paintwork, what are you having for dinner.

The aim of the exercise is to create a realisable image of the future. Creating a holistic picture with an understanding of how the dream differs from today's reality and to begin to understand the steps between now and then. This process not only generates potential solutions but creates an emotional 'anchor' to a potential future. Very often clients will generate ideas for small steps they can realistically take and some of these may end up being the goals that they set for the duration of the intervention. The exercise is drawn from SFBT and is added to by NLP from where the concept of 'anchoring' is derived.

It may seem that I have given you a lot to remember in these last two sections, the tools of MI and SFBT were described separately but you will find that in practice they become part of your repertoire of skills and if you were to later analyse a session you might find yourself using tools from both styles. They are very similar, if anything you may find that you are using more MI earlier on in an intervention.

CHAPTER 7

Working With Cards

The greatest good you can do for another is not just to share your riches, but to reveal to them their own.

Benjamin Disraeli (1804–1881)

I must say as a practitioner I love working with cards. It allows me to remember and to ask all sorts of questions. It allows clients to choose to answer or not answer. Cards help clients to feel very relaxed, to interpret things in their own way, to challenge assumptions, to acknowledge the strengths and beliefs that they hold and those of other family members. Clients often find the cards very interesting and enlightening and have sometimes asked that I leave the cards with them so that they can use them on their friends. Handing a pack of cards to a client is itself empowering.

I like to use a set of cards that look 'home made', other therapists like them to be printed, laminated and so on. This depends what you feel comfortable with. Some therapists believe that using high quality cards conveys respect for the client. I like my shabby ones because they have no authority, I believe people feel comfortable challenging them, changing them, arguing with them, ripping them up or coming up with new ones; my cards are not set in stone but are always 'works in progress'.

The most important thing is that you as a worker feel comfortable with the cards. If you feel comfortable the client is more likely to feel comfortable. If you are unsure or uneasy you will communicate that to the client. For years I used a set of cards that were blank index cards that I had written on. When I was a social work student I came across a set of 'needs' cards published by the Bridge Consultancy. I liked them so much but could not afford a set so I drew my own. Now I probably could afford a set they are out of print. These were used with parents to identify what they thought were children's needs and they helped them to discuss beliefs about homework, diet, discipline and so on. I think making your own cards is a good place to start.

For a long time I have toyed with the idea of using bigger cards and asking people in families to illustrate the concepts on them. Families often like to leave me with a memento of our time together, usually a card, a photo or a note and this would be a nice way they could help me in my work with other families.

Values cards help explore family values and validate peoples' beliefs, explore dangerous beliefs, create a cognitive dissonance and find resources that will help people change.

Strengths cards explore family and individual strengths, validating and building on people's strengths, and finding resources that will help people change.

Goal cards help to unstick some clients when having problems setting goals.

Values cards

The Values Cards help people identify and describe their most important values, thereby increasing their own self-knowledge and self-esteem. This then creates a context for goal setting and planning. When helpers have an understanding of a person's value system, they can treat them with respect and suggest ways to change or grow which is consistent with those values. Values can serve as a guide for making decisions. When people discover inconsistencies between their values and their circumstances or behaviour, a cognitive dissonance, they often are motivated to make changes. Sharing values can improve communication and understanding between people. Values often reflect the 'best' of who we are. Hope is engendered when people are encouraged to approach the change process with what is right rather than what is wrong.

Included in this set of cards are five cards with headings which are:

- Very important
- Important
- Sometimes important and sometimes not important
- Not very important
- Not at all important

The rest of the cards have the following words printed on them, you can add more if you like. I like to ask clients if they want to add more:

- Being really good at something
- Being successful
- Being part of a team
- Understanding
- Having enough time
- Competition
- Having things safe and sure
- Being myself
- Sharing

- Quiet
- Having a good relationship with god
- Taking risks
- Managing money well
- Being sober
- Being free of drugs
- Learning and growing
- Having physical strength
- Having enough money

- Allowing others to be themselves
- Being emotionally strong
- Being healthy
- Being a leader
- Living on my own
- Honesty
- Having traditions in my life
- Having a good friend, someone I can trust
- Accepting things as they are
- Being one-of-a-kind
- Having lots of interesting things to do
- Having lots of money
- Being wise
- Being effective
- Finding out what makes people 'tick'
- Being whatever and whoever I want to be
- Control
- Making people laugh
- Inner peace
- Winning
- Being well liked
- Having things
- Being a member of a family
- Helping others
- Keeping busy
- Having beautiful things around me
- Exploring old ideas

- Having a place I belong
- Excitement
- Getting along with other people
- Manipulating
- Having a comfortable home
- Having fun
- Having free time
- Fitting in
- Having a close family
- Being gentle
- Being myself
- Being the best I can be
- Making a contribution
- Having people think well of me
- Being in charge of my own life
- Doing things I'm supposed to do
- Living in harmony with others
- Having things organised
- Seeing the funny side of things
- Exploring new ideas
- Having a strong spiritual life
- Having a long happy marriage or relationship
- Power
- Living on the edge
- Having things be predictable

How to use the values cards

Introduce the cards in a non-threatening manner, this can be described as an interesting process to help clarify those things that are most important to them. Explain that there are no right or wrong answers.

Place the five category cards (Not Very Important, Not important, Sometimes Important and Sometimes Not Important, Important and Very Important) in a row in this order on a flat surface. I usually sit on the floor or at a table to do this.

Go through the rest of the cards and ask the person to place each value card in a category. Ask them to use their first 'gut' reaction when deciding how to categorise a card. They should define each word as they wish (don't encourage use of a dictionary and don't offer your definition). If a word has no particular meaning to them, have them just set that card aside. Encourage the person to add any values that are important but not included in the deck.

Take time to discuss and clarify the individual's response to each card and to reflect the positive things that clients are finding to say about themselves. Some people may want more time and privacy, give them as much time and privacy as desired.

When all cards have been sorted, ask the person to select the six top values from the 'Very Important' pile (six is not a magic number, it's simply an easy number of things for people to hold in their heads. Five or seven is fine. The point is to select a small number of 'Core Values').

Have the individual prioritise their six core values from first to sixth.

Finally, have the person define each one using their own words. We suggest the final list of core values and their definitions be put in writing and left with the person for future use. Sometimes this written feedback can be quite elaborate and an example of this is included on the next page.

This is a very gentle process. It is not an opportunity to pry and lever information out of clients. It is an opportunity for them to express themselves. It should be fun and easy to do and not at all challenging for the client. This exercise should not leave the client feeling exposed or pressured, it should however help to build a rapport between you and the client at this early stage.

With some clients the exercise can take as much as two hours to complete. At the end of it clients will often feel that they have expressed their feelings about what they believe in, you will both feel that you know a lot more about each other you will have built an atmosphere of respect and trust.

Following on from this exercise I will take their top six cards back to my office and take the time to write a positive and reflective statement about the exercise. I usually print it out on some nice paper and give it back to them at the next session. Below is some written feedback from a past client – of course his name has been changed.

Example of written feedback from value cards

John is a quiet man who wants to be in charge of his own life. He strives to be the best person he can be. The best father he can be, the best husband and lover he can be.

John feels it is very important to have fun. He does this on his own and with his family. He wants to give his children a fun time so that they can develop into well balanced young people who enjoy life. John understands that it is important for him to have fun so that he has space for himself. He is able to let off steam and feel relaxed so that he has energy to work for his family's happiness.

He works hard to be in charge of his own life. He feels that it is important to constantly learn and grow. John is creative and interested in new ideas and new ways of doing things.

John feels the most important thing to him is inner peace. He feels that by having a balanced life, having fun, being in charge of his own life, learning and growing and constantly trying to be the best person he can be is the path to his inner peace.

This exercise represents a rare opportunity for the client to discuss and validate what they believe about family life. It will be seen that the statements on all of the cards are positive so the client has little choice but to express these values positively.

Because the statements will all be positive, the feedback is often aspirational, it represents how the individual sees him or herself when they are at their best. We are not talking necessarily about how the client behaves, we are discussing their values and so they are telling us how their beliefs tell them they should behave, again we have a Cognitive Dissonance.

Strength cards

This set of cards provides people with an enjoyable method of identifying their individual strengths, interests and resources that can be used to solve problems and achieve goals.

Interventions are most successful when they build on existing strengths; however, people often are not able to identify their own strengths and resources, especially during times of crisis. These cards are one method to elicit a list of strengths. You are encouraged to suggest some strengths you've seen in clients as they do these cards. People also may feel better about working with professionals and other helpers, and thus more capable of change, knowing that the helper appreciates their strengths.

Like the Values cards I have a set of strengths card that I print out on plain paper and cut out. They are just pieces of paper that people can write on if they want. There are a variety of professionally made packs of strengths cards available, some from the Brief Therapy Practice. They have different kinds of headings and contents but the main point is that you work with clients to expose and agree that the client has some useful strengths. Clients are often visibly lifted at the end of a session with cards.

On my cards there are headings followed by suggestions about what those headings mean, you can of course add others if you wish.

Sexuality

What are the things about your sexuality that you like? Think about such things as having a partner, safe sex, no diseases, no abuse, pregnancy issues etc.

Cleanliness as a strength

What are the things around you that are clean and free from germs? Think about odours, dust, toys etc.

Drugs and alcohol

How do you and your family stay away from drugs you feel are unhelpful? What are the drugs your family members are choosing not to use? What drugs are you choosing to use that are helpful?

Relationships

Think about your friends and family. Who do you have relationships with that are pleasing to you? Who would you go to when you needed to talk about something important to you? Who helps you out when you need it?

Household items

Think about the things around your home which you like. Think about safe household items. Think about appliances, furniture, decorations and other such things.

Transportation

How do you get around? What are the transport resources you can use at this time? What other transport resources are there if you need them?

Health services

Is your family healthy? What do you like about your family's health care?

Finances

What do you do well to handle your money? Do you have enough money for needed things? Do you have enough money for extra things? What ways have you tried to earn extra money?

Sleep strengths

What do you like about your sleep patterns? Are you getting enough sleep? Do you have a comfortable and quiet place to sleep?

Physical characteristics which are strengths

As you think about yourself and your body, what do you like? Think about strength, endurance, agility, exercise, health etc.

Physical environment

What are the things in your home and neighbourhood which you like? Think of noise, temperature, electricity, water, lighting etc.

Animals

What pets or wild animals are around you which you like? What do you like about those animals?

Skills

Tell me some of the skills which you are proud of? Make a list of things you do well. Think of things including recreation, interpersonal skills, household, creative and professional skills.

Chemicals not available to children

Are your children safe from chemicals such as petrol fumes, drugs, cleaners and poisons. How are they protected from them?

Child safety

What are the things present or absent which make your children safe. Think of the area you live in, streets, food, school, drugs, safety from others, people who look out for them.

Nutrition

Are you and your family eating well? Are you eating enough? Think about the kinds of food you eat. Are they healthy? How much do you know about healthy eating?

Adult safety

How safe do you feel? What do you do to make sure that you and others around you are safe? Think about your own actions to help keep things safe. How do the actions of others keep you safe?

Spirituality

Think about your sense of values, belonging, goals, religion, belief in a higher power. What do you see as your strengths in this area? What resources are available to help you with this part of your life?

Children's school issues

What do you like about your children's school? Think about the school activities, transport, attendance, friends etc.

Adult education

What resources are there to help you to get further education?

Moods

Think about all of your moods. Which moods do you have which you consider your strengths? Describe how well you handle moods which will create negative feelings.

Spaces

As you think about your living environment, what do you like about it? Include your home, the area you live in, open spaces, parks. Shopping etc. What about your environment is it that is safe and pleasing?

Appearance

What do you like about your appearance? What resources are available to you to maintain or improve your appearance?

There are commercially available strength cards, mainly from the Brief Therapy Practice, contact details are at the end of the manual.

How to use the strength cards

Talking about strengths can be a potentially discouraging discussion for people who are feeling overwhelmed by problems and hard pressed to come up with any positives about themselves. These cards are meant to be used in a positive way (never interrogate or put someone 'on the spot'). Here are some suggestions:

1   Do it individually. To start a casual discussion, you might say, 'This is an activity to get us started thinking about all the things that are going right in our lives. Sometimes when we have problems, they're all we think about and we tend to forget the good things or take them for granted. All people have special areas of strength, and I'm thinking that as we talk we'll discover strengths you have that you can use to make some of the changes you want.' Then go through each card together, being sure to point out strengths you've observed about which the person may not have thought.

2   Do it as a family activity. Each member takes a turn drawing a card, and describes a strength they have in that particular area. If they can't think of one (or even if they can), other family members can point out a strength that the individual has in that area. You could even make a game out of it: the family member earns 2 points for identifying a strength of their own and 1 point for identifying the strength of others in the family. It's a game everyone wins!

3   Write down all the strengths that come up, and keep the list to refer to when problem solving.

4   Make a bright poster listing all the strengths, to serve as a daily visual reminder that 'I am a strong person with lots of assets' or, some other creative way to help apply the strengths while you work together.

5   Talk about areas that the client or family want to strengthen.

Goal cards

The goal cards help people:

- Take a broad look at hundreds of factors impacting their lives.
- Identify and prioritise needs they have.
- Set specific goals to work toward.

The act of identifying needs and setting goals is motivating in itself, and research tells us that when people set their own goals they are more likely to follow through on them (people don't work on problems they don't have!) and maintain progress once the goal is reached.

The very act of handing a person the goal cards is empowering. It says, in effect 'This is your life. You are in charge of deciding how to live it. You are capable of making good choices. I have confidence in you!' Since the process emphasises capacity of the individual rather than worker expertise, it gives the message that the person can make changes and will be given credit for those changes. A person's confidence and motivation tends to increase with the knowledge that someone else believes in their ability.

The goal cards list hundreds of factors that interact to impact human health and well-being. When people take a systematic look through these cards, it gives them the opportunity to think about a wide range of issues that may have an impact on their situation. This can be especially helpful during times of crisis, when people tend to focus exclusively on one or two problems, but haven't considered the 'big picture'. This process helps people discover how seemingly unrelated factors in their lives are connected; in other words, it helps them to think holistically about their life.

With these cards, individuals identify and prioritise factors they would like to work on in order to change their lives for the better. They set specific and meaningful goals. The process structures setting small goals, many of which will be readily achievable, leading to more success, which will enhance both their confidence and motivation for further change. A person can continue to use this simple assessment tool on their own any time goals are reached or circumstances change.

How to use the goal cards

How to introduce this exercise depends a lot on the particular person and work setting, so be creative in making it work for you. I often leave these cards with the client as 'homework' and ask them to circle or highlight the goals they would like to work on. There are 26 cards altogether, each with a heading and a number of choices for the client to make. Here are some more ideas about how to use them:

- When the person has stated a goal, but before beginning much work toward it:
  Let's do this exercise before we go any further, to make sure we haven't forgotten anything and are seeing the big picture.

- After making headway on initial goals:
  We've done a lot! What I'd like to do now is an exercise to see where else I could be helpful to you – what other areas we could give attention to for the next two weeks.

- When it's all chaos:
  You've a lot on your mind – here's a tool that can help make things clearer and give us a better idea what to start working on first.

- When crisis after crisis happens:
  Here's a tool that helps us get a little distance from what's happening right now – puts this crisis in perspective, and gives us some idea about what we can do to prevent this kind of thing from happening again.

The cards

Substance abuse

I would like to:

Prevent access to buying drink or drugs
Control drinking or drugs
Reduce drinking or drug use
Stop drinking or using drugs
Make friends with those who don't drink or use drugs
Help kids not to drink or use drugs
Stop smoking

Take care of health problems
Comply with legal requirements
Improve relationships damaged by drinking or drugs
Learn drink or drug-free ways of living
Get medical help
Comply with court orders
Other

Health

I would like to:

Reduce headaches
Reduce backaches
Reduce stomach-aches
Reduce accidents
Reduce injuries
Reach my desired weight
Practice safe sex
Get enough exercise
Manage high blood pressure
Cope with allergies

Increase energy
Get a pregnancy test
Get birth control
Reduce pain
Protect against AIDS
Address physical problems to do with: heart, digestive system, skin, eyes, hearing, muscles, bones etc.
Other

Health care

I would like to:

Get vaccinations
Get emergency care
Have a physical examination
Have a gynaecological examination
Get pre-natal care
Get a regular doctor
Get help with long-term medical problems

Have access to counselling/mental health care
Stop throwing up
Overcome eating disorders
Prevent disease
Other

Moods

I would like to:

Manage my anger
Reduce frustration
Reduce anxiety
Experience joy
Decrease loneliness
Begin to feel emotions
Feel happier
Feel less confused
Relax
Be affectionate
Feel wanted
Experience excitement
Feel needed
Feel worthwhile
Feel less overwhelmed

Stay calm
Develop courage
Manage mood swings
Feel less afraid
Be loving
Rome from foster care
Keep kids out of foster care
Get clarity on what abuse is
Prepare for court hearings
Get clarity on what neglect is
Know when and how to intervene
Provide clothing
Provide meals regularly
Other

School

I would like to help my child:

Get along with teachers
Improve grades
Reduce fighting
Behave well
Cope with hyperactivity
Participate in sports

Learn study skills
Learn to read
Get back into school
Cope with learning disabilities
Do extracurricular activities

I would like to:

Get involved with my kids' schooling
Get school clothes

Other

Relationships

I would like to:

Identify shared values
Find common interests
Spend quality family time
Spend time with friends
Find a good partner
Improve social skills
Develop real friendships
Rebuild relationships
Create a happy marriage
Get along at work
Get along at college

Get along with neighbour
Find someone I can count on
Develop problem-solving abilities
Find someone to talk to about things that
    worry me
Find someone who accepts my children, no
    matter how they act
Begin or continue family traditions
Have good relationships with family
members
Other

Housework

I would like to:

Pay bills
Store cleaners safely
Get help with the shopping
Clean car
Store toys
Clean yard or garden
Get help with cooking
Clean kitchen
Vacuum

Clean up rubbish
Get help with laundry
Develop routines
Clean kids' rooms
Clean living room
Get help with chores
Clean bathroom
Have kids help with the housework
Other

Personal growth and fulfilment

I would like to:

Find inner peace

Clarify personal values

Become active

Feel hopeful

Get more education

Travel

Plan for the future

Get motivation

Become organised

Develop career goals

Feel like I belong

Get married

Have a big family

Be myself

Learn a skill

Have a small family

Stay single

Be more open-minded

Learn to make wise decisions

Become independent

Develop a sense of meaning for my life

Develop a vision of the future

Put my spiritual beliefs into practice

Get more education

Other

Furnishings

I would like to:

Find or repair furniture or appliances, including:

Stove/cooker

Cribs

Refrigerator

Tables

Heater

Chairs

Phone

Sofas

Washer

Dressers

Dryer

Beds

Plumbing

Other

Money and bills

I would like to:

Get ongoing income

Pay off debts

Apply for benefits

Get help with debts

Get money for rent

Borrow money

Get help with bills

Stick to a budget

Have enough money for basic needs

Save money

Cope with collection agencies

Have enough money for extras

Learn to negotiate with creditors

Other

Legal issues

I would like to:

Go to court
Deal with lawsuits
Guard against threats
Retain or get custody
Get a divorce
Deal with debt collectors
Learn about adoption
Learn about residency order

Learn about care order
Explore counselling programme
Complete community service
Get protection from violent/abusive person
Find legal services
Comply with probation/court orders
Other

Clothes

I would like to:

Find laundry facilities
Decide on appropriate clothing
Get clothes for work
Get kids' clothes
Get coats

Get shoes
Have fashionable clothes
Find clothes I feel good in
Other

Dental care

I would like to:

Schedule checkups
Get rid of toothache
Decrease headaches
Decrease stiff neck
Have cavities filled

Get braces
Buy toothpaste and toothbrushes
Learn to care for teeth
Other

Appearance

I would like to:

Improve my skin
Buy clothes
Improve my hair
Care for clothes
Reach ideal weight
Improve image
Fix teeth

Take time for grooming
Strengthen muscles
Improve hygiene
Learn how to use makeup
Learn how to style hair
Other

Exercise and fun

I would like to:

Find a hobby
Spend time with friends
Find recreational facilities
Make friends
Join a team
Take lessons/join a class
Play with kids
Prevent injuries
Play games/sports
Do aerobics/yoga/gym
Garden

Draw
Care for injuries
Get appropriate clothing
Find time to exercise
Increase stamina
Schedule enjoyable family time
Become stronger
Get equipment
Participate in activities: fishing, reading, swimming, jogging, walking, hiking, skating, rowing, basketball, handball

Daily routines

I would like to:

Keep up with the housework
Keep up with commitments
Get enough sleep
Make time to exercise
Schedule time for fun
Spend time with partner
Have time to relax
Spend time with each child
Have time for myself

Make regular meals
Complete housework
Keep up with laundry
Spend family time
Make grooming routines
Spend time with friends
Make and keep appointments
Keep up with correspondence
Learn that it is okay to say 'No'

Sexuality

I would like to:

Prevent AIDS
Get reliable birth control
Explore sexual identity
Find a partner
Improve my sex life
Leave an abusive partner
Educate my kids about sex
Protect against sexual abuse

Prevent sexually transmitted diseases
Get pre-natal care
Deal with unwanted pregnancy
Find the best method of birth control
Get treatment for sexually transmitted disease
Other

Past abuse and trauma

I would like to recover from events in my past, specifically:

Sexual abuse
Rape
War
Physical abuse
Incest
Suicide
Loss of a loved one
Abortion
Miscarriage
Domestic violence
Death of a child

Crime
Loss of a home
Fire or explosions
Divorce
Loss of a job
Natural disasters
Emotional abuse
Loss of a child to foster care
Loss of a close friend
Other

Child or teen behaviour

I would like to help my child:

Find a job
Attend school
Stay safe
Reduce lying
Learn respect
Reduce arguing
Reduce stealing
Be toilet trained
Learn about safer sex
Reduce yelling
Help with chores
Improve grades
Obey house rules
Reduce swearing
Learn responsibility

Learn social skills
Get along with peers
Get along with adults
Stop or avoid alcohol
Learn to disagree
Cope with hyperactivity
Stop or avoid smoking
Reduce talking back
Stop or avoid using drugs
Stop or avoid running away
Learn how to manage money
Learn how to implement family values
Care for possessions
Other

Transport

I would like to:

Repair car
Buy a car
Use car seat
Get bus pass
Use bus
Use seat belts
Learn to drive
Use taxi service

Walk
Use ferry
Use train
Get baby buggy
Get baby carrier
Hitchhike
Buy motorcycle
Get driver's licence

Transport (continued)

Use subway
Fix brakes
Use boat
Use life jackets

Use bicycle
Ride with friends or relatives
Other

Rest and relaxation

I would like to:
Get enough privacy
Get enough sleep
Get enough exercise
Find time to rest
Get bedding
Worry less
Reduce interruptions
Have peace and quiet

Get a comfortable bed
Have my own space
Reduce pain
Learn relaxation techniques
Get help with house work
Schedule time for myself
Other

Food

I would like to:
Shop wisely
Get help with cooking
Cope with allergies
Get pet food
Plan appetising meals
Stick to a healthy diet

Reach healthy weight
Learn to cook
Learn about nutrition
Get enough healthy food
Learn budgeting skills
Other

Adult education

I would like to:
Get education
Get job training
Earn a diploma or degree
Improve reading skills
Attend parenting classes

Attend anger control classes
Find time and money to attend
Attend community education classes for fun
Other

Child care

I would like to:

Find nearby child care

Find drop-in child care

Find affordable child care

Find weekend child care

Find night-time child care

Get help to pay for child care

Find after-school child care

Use family or friends for child care

Learn about child development

Learn to evaluate caregivers for safety

Get reliable transportation to and from child care

Other

Blank card. Write in the goals that are important to you

I would like to:

Download your cards

If you take a look at my website *www.another-way.co.uk* you will find sets of cards that you can just download, print and cut out with scissors. I tend to use different coloured paper for each set of cards so that I can identify them easily, yellow for values, pink for strengths and blue for goals.

I must give thanks here to Doug and Soledad from Homebuilders in the USA who provided us with these cards (and lots of other ideas), and gave us permission to reproduce them. The cards are occasionally changed or added to by practitioners and families so do not be surprised if the cards you download are slightly different from the cards in the book. They are still used in the same way.

CHAPTER 8

Paper Exercises

We cannot teach people anything; we can only help them to discover it for themselves.

Galileo (1564–1642)

In this section we will look at some paper exercises including the safety plan which we do with the family within the first 72 hours, Goal Attainment Scaling, how we set, prioritise and clarify goals and the Weekly Plan which helps the worker to plan the intervention.

Creating a safety plan

Within the first 72 hours, together with the family we will be devising a safety plan if this is appropriate. We would do this if there is some behaviour in the family that could case harm to a child immediately. For instance, drinking and domestic violence, dangerous home conditions or other immediate risks.

It is vital that the plan is devised by the family and not by the therapist. The therapist needs to be sensitive when coming up with ideas as the family may just accept them. They need to be fully engaged in the process and devise a plan that they feel is realistic and are motivated to stick to.

A case example is used here to illustrate how the safety plan is used:

Peter and Karen

This is extracted from a real case taken from our files. Some details have been changed to maintain confidentiality.

Peter and Karen were both drinkers and the police were often being called because of violence in the home. Each parent had in the past hospitalised the other. Social workers had placed the children on the CPR for emotional abuse and were considering removing them from the home due to the ongoing level of drinking and violence.

Early in the intervention Karen stated that one of her concerns was that one of the children was becoming more violent and difficult to control.

Both parents had as children themselves experienced backgrounds of domestic violence. They both agreed that they did not wish to subject their children to similar experiences, nor did they wish to lose them to the local authority. I asked them to tell me about what their lives were like as children. What did their childhood feel like? How did they behave and why? What did they want to do? How did they cope? They felt that their violent, drunk and verbally abusive parents gave them a bad start and still affected them in many ways today. There were lots of tears at this session.

I asked the parents to describe the effects of their parents' behaviour on them and they were able to come up with a list including:

- Going off the rails.

- Being depressed or frightened.

- Lacking confidence.

- Lack of success in the future because of this.

- Lack of close family ties.

This was a real 'lightbulb moment' for this couple and they were able to talk about how their behaviour may be having the same effect on their own children. Peter and Karen were able to be clear that their behaviour, although it sometimes felt uncontrollable, was a risk to the children's emotional wellbeing.

Karen and Peter had lost a ten year old son to an illness some time before and much of their behaviour was related to grief and anger and an inability to communicate this to the partner. We looked at these issues separately.

I asked Peter and Karen to look at what they could do to achieve their goal of protecting the children from the effects of their grief and anger. They came up with a plan which was intended to be a short term agreement by both parties, to protect the children while we addressed the communication issues. The plan was intended to last about a week. However it was still being used a year later.

Both parents felt that sometimes they could recognise the early signs of loss of control in the other person and decided to use trigger words that they would both agree to abide by when they noticed that behaviour. They agreed that if one of them felt things were getting out of control they would say 'we need to stop this now' and the other person would respect that, even if they felt it was unfair, and leave the room for a short period.

If you look at the plan, you will see that it begins with a brief analysis of risks and strengths. You can see how the plan is set in the context of their beliefs and values about their family and uses the strengths they talked about. The risks are described in a clear factual way without emotional content, there is no potential to argue for different interpretations or for one partner to unfairly blame the other. The plan itself leaves no opportunity for alternate interpretations. A copy of the plan is sent to the referrer with the 72 hour report.

We would always use the same four headings for the different sections of the plan, exploring risks and strengths, identifying behaviours and who is to respond to that behaviour and what they do in response. The practice of speaking about these risks openly and clearly and the strengths that can be used to deal with them is often the very first acknowledgement that the family members have some power to make things change.

Creating a safety plan

Adult family members: Peter Watson, Karen Watson.
Child family members: Michael Watson, Stephen Jones, Robert Watson.

Risks present	Strengths in the family
■ Peter has been physically violent to Karen. ■ Karen has been physically violent to Peter. ■ Peter has been verbally violent to Karen. ■ Karen has been verbally violent to Peter. ■ The children have been present during some of these incidents. ■ Alcohol has often played a part in the verbal and physical violence between Karen and Peter. ■ The children are becoming violent. ■ There is a risk that the children may be removed from their family.	■ Peter and Karen have a strong belief in the importance of family. ■ Peter and Karen have supportive relationships in the area. ■ Peter and Karen are committed to staying together and to making things better. ■ Karen has been able to say that she can not safely drink alcohol. ■ Peter and Karen have been able to say that their relationship has been violent and they want it to stop. ■ Peter and Karen are both aware of the effect that verbal and physical violence had on them as children.

Plan

When	Who and What
1. **Karen** finds herself losing her temper	**Peter** will repeat the trigger words 'We need to stop now' **Peter** will look after the children **Karen** will go to her room
2. When **Peter** feels himself losing his temper	**Karen** will repeat the trigger words 'We need to stop now' **Karen** will look after the children. **Peter** will leave the house and stay at Martin's
3. If **Karen** has more than two drinks	**Karen** will go home and go to bed.

Signed:

Goal attainment scaling (GAS)

Goal attainment scaling was first developed in the 1960s by mental health services in Minnesota, USA. They were looking for a measuring device that was flexible enough to allow a wide variety of individualised problem definition, allowed each client to set his own definition of 'success', would indicate a magnitude of success or failure and would allow interpretable comparison between different interventions. See Kiresuk and Lund (1976).

GAS is a five point scale of individualised potential outcomes, placing the target goal in the centre of the range of possible outcomes. GAS is a flexible structure that can accommodate a wide variety of measures. It is an advantage that the client is measured only on dimensions that are relevant to him. Another advantage is that a meaningful range of values is chosen.

GAS has clear benefit for clients. The client is clearly aware of his target goal; he has been guided to be clear about what that target behaviour looks like. Yet he is also clear what an improvement on his stated goal would look like and what less than success would look like. This gives the client an understanding that improvement can continue and also that improvement is not a question of right or wrong, but is a spectrum forever changing. The client therefore has a feeling of control and direction and an ability to forgive his mistakes and get back on track.

The process itself is highly motivational for clients. It focusses them on success, it allows them to define their own success, it confers the belief that success is attainable; it validates their personal beliefs and goals.

If Goal Sheets are completed with the full control of the client, they can become highly personal items which reflect a sense of self efficacy. Clients should of course have their own copies of all paper exercises that we do with them.

1. Selecting goals

The first step in selection of a goal involves identifying problem areas. On the goal sheet, make a brief statement of the problem trying to be as behaviourally specific as possible.

This problem is then re-stated into a goal. It is important to state a positive goal (e.g. increased school attendance) rather than a negative goal (e.g. decreased truancy). Obviously you and the client may have many more goals than can be addressed during the intervention. Only scale those goals that you and the client have determined to be priorities during the intervention.

You should ideally have at least one goal during the first week of the intervention. Additional goals may be formulated at any time. Usually a therapist and client formulate between two and four goals per participating individual in the family.

2. Importance

The second step is the assignment of a numerical weight to each goal, how important is it? Weight may be a number from 1 to 10 and should reflect the relative importance of the goal areas. This helps to prioritise which goals are to be worked on first and provides the opportunity to negotiate goal priorities with the client and helps the client to be clear about the importance of this change.

3. Statement of target outcome '0' level

This involves clearly stating an outcome that is expected for each goal. Take into account the timescale for this goal. Is it something that can be done in four weeks or is it a longer term goal involving the support of another agency.

This middle level represents the most probable level of goal attainment. The goal must be stated so that two independent observers could agree on whether it has been attained.

Some goals are observable in themselves – (e.g. 'Has not drunk for the past month') and can usually be determined by talking to the client or another informant. Other goals may require separate attainment criteria (e.g. reduced depression would probably demand a behavioural indicator such as the client is able to sleep eight uninterrupted hours each night). In stating the expected outcome it should be remembered that the criteria of outcome will have to be consistent throughout the balance on the scale, each level should clearly signpost the next level. Scoring is easier if each outcome is defined by concrete behaviours that can be directly observed or reported.

4. Completion of the other scale levels

Using the 'expected outcome' as a benchmark, the next task is to complete the four remaining outcome levels on the scale. The two adjacent cells represent less possible outcomes. A completed scale should contain five mutually exclusive levels and represent an exhaustive and internally consistent continuum of possible outcomes in relation to the particular goal. In practice it is sometimes adequate to define the expected outcomes and at least one of the levels above and one below the expected outcome.

After scaling, go back and review the scale to determine if it contains errors that may make follow up scoring difficult. Three kinds of error in particular should be avoided:

- **Vagueness**. Scales should be specific enough so that at least two independent follow up scorers could agree on which level best describes the client.

- **Multiple dimensions**. Scales should contain only one criterion variable so that differential change along two or more dimensions will not confuse follow up.

- **Incompleteness**. All five outcome levels should be clearly implied by the three or four cells completed.

5. Terminating and scoring a goal

The last step in the use of goal attainment scaling is scoring. Scoring simply involves determining which outcome level best describes a client at the time the goal is scored and indicating this on the goal sheet. Each goal may be scored only at one level, indicating that attainment was at least at that level but not up to the next one. It is permissible to score a goal between levels (i.e. a scored 1.5 is okay).

A goal is scored at the time it is devised with the client and then again at the end of the intervention. It is then scored again on the follow up record sheet and statistical sheets (see Appendix) at the follow up visits to the family at one, three, six and twelve months after the end of the intervention.

The following pages include a number of goal sheets that have been completed.

Goal sheet

Family Name: Smith   **Therapist:** Mark
Goal #1

Statement of problem (*This statement must be behaviourally specific to what has been observed or reported*)

All of the children have their names on the CPR under the category of neglect. School attendance has been erratic. Although he feels the two things are not linked, Richard smokes heroin and would like to stop, he would like to try a methadone reduction programme.

Date goal scaled: 02 Jan 2004   **Date when scored:** 02 Feb 2004
Rating when scaled: −2   **Rating when scored:** −1
Whose goal: Richard
Importance: 10/10

Most unfavourable outcome thought likely (**−2**)	Richard continues to use street drugs.
Less than expected level of success (**−1**)	Richard starts on methadone but continues to use heroin or other street drugs occasionally.
On target, expected level of success (**0**)	Richard is not using heroin or other street drugs. He is stable on Methadone.
More than expected level of success (**+1**)	Richard does not use heroin or other street drugs and is reducing his use of substitutes.
Best anticipated success (**+2**)	Richard does not use street drugs or substitutes.

Goal sheet

Family name: Smith   **Therapist:** Mark
Goal #2

Statement of problem (*This statement must be behaviourally specific to what has been observed or reported*)

All of the children have their names on the CPR under the category of neglect. School attendance has been erratic and Richard wants the children to have the best chances of success in the future so he wants the children to attend school and not waste their lives.

Date goal scaled: 02 Jan 2004   **Date when scored:** 02 Feb 2004
Rating when scaled: -1 **Rating when scored:** 0
Whose Goal: Richard
Importance: 10/10

Most unfavourable outcome thought likely ($-$**2**)	The children miss so much school they seriously damage their future.
Less than expected level of success ($-$**1**)	The children avoid going to school when it suits them and so damage their chances of success in the future.
On Target, Expected level of success (**0**)	Richard ensures that the children go to school every day and so learn new skills and that will help them to achieve their goals in the future.
More than expected level of success ($+$**1**)	
Best anticipated success ($+$**2**)	The children participate in organised after school activities.

Goal sheet

Family name: Smith   **Therapist:** Mark
Goal #3

Statement of problem (*This statement must be behaviourally specific to what has been observed or reported*)

Social Services are concerned that Janet and Richard have missed appointments with professionals, this has caused them to put pressure on the couple. Richard and Janet feel that they need to be more organised and have more harmony in their lives.

Date goal scaled: 02 Jan 2004   **Date when scored:** 02 Feb 2004
Rating when scaled: −2   **Rating when scored:** 0
Whose goal: Richard
Importance: 10/10

Most unfavourable outcome thought likely (**−2**)	Some appointments are missed and others are unprepared for. The family suffers stress and disharmony. Social Services continue to put pressure on and this makes the family feel worse.
Less than expected level of success (**−1**)	Richard uses a calendar but sometimes forgets to record appointments or to look at it. Still chaotic and stressful. Social Services still putting the pressure on.
On target, expected level of success (**0**)	Richard keeps all appointments with professionals. When clashes happen that he was not expecting, he contacts the professionals as soon as he becomes aware of the problem and changes the appointment. A bit of a drag but it saves a lot of hassle. Social Services have nothing to complain about.
More than expected level of success (**+1**)	Richard does not miss any appointments. He is always ready, always prepared for appointments. Much less stress. Much more harmony. No nasty surprises.
Best anticipated success (**+2**)	

Result of behaviour-specific goal setting

- Reduces confusion

- Specifies and clarifies problems

- Avoids blame

- Allows clients to prioritise

- Inspires hope in clients and therapist

- Helps generate treatment options

- Frames goals that appear reachable

- Allows monitoring and evaluation

- Allows re-examination and changes

- Explores practical and ecological barriers to change

- Allows client and therapist to develop a family centred plan of action

Developing a family centred plan of action

Each individual in the family will have devised their own goals and there will be a separate sheet for each of these goals. This is now a time for planning the next part of the intervention, what new skills or resources do people need in order to progress toward their goals?

- In partnership, helper and family members establish the action steps to achieve the goal.

- Steps are best broken down into their smallest components.

- Determine the family's ability to develop a small plan, with only a few steps at a time or can they develop a more detailed plan of many steps over a longer period.

- Understand 'What are the barriers that would keep you from achieving your goal during the time we are together'.

- Brainstorm options for handling the barriers and reaching goals:
  - ☐ Removing some barriers.
  - ☐ Going around some barriers.
  - ☐ Learning to cope with some barriers which cannot be removed or circumvented.

- Weighing pros and cons of all options or methods for action.

- Choosing and prioritising options or methods.

- Selecting tasks for now until the next visit, and who will do them, and when.

- Identifying and choosing resources to help accomplish the options selected.

- Review change process and expectations. By itself the commitment to change cannot instantly transport families to the journey's ultimate destination, families must take the journey of change themselves.

- Review coping strategies, progress on goals, strengths, values, overall health and well-being and family's picture of a new life.

- Help them address how the options affect the entire family, not just the individual working on a goal if it is an individual goal.

The weekly plan

A useful tool for the therapist at this point is to write down the tasks into a weekly plan.

A 'classic' weekly plan would have the first week focussing on getting to understand the family and its members through reflective listening, then moving into developing and clarifying goals in the first week. Looking at practical barriers to change and how these can be removed.

The second week would be about teaching and practising new skills which will help family members to achieve their goals, the final two weeks would focus on practice, practice, practice.

Each family member would have their own goals. Some of their goals might be the same, Richard and Janet in the examples may have all their goals in common, but they would still have separate goal sheets. Sometimes goals will be very different and may even conflict. In this case the therapists would have to create an environment where a way through that conflict could be negotiated.

Weekly plan

Client name: Richard, Janet, Colin and Wendy Smith.
Clinical social worker: Mark Hamer

Week 1

- Reflectively listen to family members.

- Explore and clarify their goals.

- Positively reinforce their strengths and self motivational statements.

- Make referrals for Richard and Janet to Community Addictions unit with a view to starting a reducing methadone programme.

- Look at what needs to be done to help Richard and Janet with their shared goal of getting the children to school every day.

- Get alarm clock.

- Work with whole family to explore what life will be like when parents have made the changes they want to make.

- Work with children Colin and Wendy on how they feel about going to school every day.

- What will the difficulties be and what will help them to overcome these?

- Help Richard and Janet to use a calendar and negotiate their way out of clashing appointments.

Week 2

- Explore what changes Janet and Richard can make now that will help them to deal with life without heroin.

- Teach practical parenting skills re: managing the children's resistance to going to school.

- Teach Janet and Richard relaxation skills.

- Help them to develop alternative routines (adult education – gym?)

- Teach and practice positive self talk.

- Devise crisis card.

Week 3

- Practice parenting skills.

- Practice relaxation.

- Practice positive self talk.

- Teach and practice use of crisis card.

- Discuss and identify further goals.

- Identify future intervention – agree other appropriate services – make referrals.

Week 4

- Practice parenting skills.

- Practice relaxation.

- Practice positive self talk.

- Review and practice use of crisis card.

CHAPTER 9

Teaching New Skills

The greatest revolution of our generation is the discovery that human beings, by changing the inner attitudes of their minds, can change the outer aspects of their lives.

William James, Psychologist (1842–1910)

Our role once clients have identified and set their goals, is to teach people new skills. It is important that our clients learn how to learn and are able to adapt to changing circumstances long after we have gone. We want people to learn how to get by with less pain, more happiness, less arguing, more accomplishments and more fun!

Workers may need to overcome any barriers to learning that the family might have. These might include low self-esteem or lack of confidence, being preoccupied with other more important things, a belief that it is not worth it, that there is no point or that they are unable to learn anything new.

Providing support services

Families are often concerned with basic issues like food and housing. Because of this their emotions might be out of control and they will be unable to apply themselves to learning new skills. If we are working with clients who cannot provide food for their children because they have no electricity or cooker, if the children have no bedding; or if the roof leaks, then clients are not going to be able to concentrate on anything else until those needs are met. Mothers are unlikely to be able to reward their children for good behaviour if they are preoccupied with finding food. Children will not be able to concentrate in school if they are mocked for being smelly or having holey shoes (Berg, 2000).

Our role in such situations clearly would be to look at issues around income and expenditure; but before that we may need to remove a barrier to learning new skills. We may have to provide concrete services ourselves such as buying a cooker, shoes, gas or electricity. We hold a small budget for each family which is easily accessible to the worker. Sometimes we use it and sometimes we don't so we can roll it over to new clients and from time to time afford to buy larger items.

We may have to provide money sometimes but ideally when we have to provide such services we would do as little as possible and get families to do as much as possible.

We can learn a lot from watching clients and take advantage of teachable moments when we share tasks such as shopping. Spending time on such tasks shows us how they fit into the whole pattern of a person's life. We can also provide services such as emergency transport as most therapists have cars. We would not want to provide routine transport as we would want to teach and encourage families to learn how to use systems normally available to them.

We would work with the family to help them to identify resources available to them and if necessary work with them to enable them to develop the personal or social skills which would allow them to access such resources.

Learning

Families may believe that change happens by a worker 'fixing' something or that it is not possible to change or to learn. Families may feel that learning is irrelevant, that being happy is not possible or that learning anything new is too hard.

We want to make failure impossible. We are often working people who have little formal education, we want them to feel that they can succeed and we want them to notice their success. We do this by making the steps to their goals so small that they cannot fail. We acknowledge that learning can be difficult but we try to make learning as rewarding and as fun as possible. We will give rewards; verbal or material for attempts in the right direction.

Worker skills

Workers need to be functioning at a high level. They need to be able to facilitate negotiation between people who are experiencing high emotional levels. They will certainly have experience of working with families in crisis in their own homes and they will be able to keep themselves up to date with current thinking and research.

Workers need to be patient and caring, accepting of different styles and paces of learning, 'the mediocre teacher tells, the good teacher explains, the superior teacher demonstrates and the great teacher inspires' (William Arthur Ward). The worker often has to learn new skills or access other resources, e.g. what is current best practice in working with agoraphobia? What practical resources will enable them to get their children to school on time? What is helpful for people who self harm? What services are accessible for this client who needs to detox?

The following pages contain ideas for teaching new skills which may be useful. Many of them are given without instructions or explanation, you will need to use your own creativity to exploit them, some can be used as handouts that can be copied and given to clients.

Inevitably this section only holds a few ideas but they can be added to by the worker as they come across other useful tools.

If people do come across tools and ideas that they feel other workers or families would find useful, please contact me through the website (*www.another-way.co.uk*), including details about where the tool came from.

Crisis cards

This is a tool that clients can use when in crisis to help them to identify alternative ways of coping rather than reverting to behaviours which have caused problems. This could be used to help feelings associated with anger, depression, agoraphobia, or cravings to drink or use drugs. Clients learn about developing crisis cards in several stages – these can occur in one visit.

Crisis cards are designed to divert escalating feelings by having clients act before their feelings get out of control. We will talk with clients about feelings and levels of feelings. We usually begin by identifying end points. I might ask a client to tell me about a time when everything was fantastic, when they felt as good as they could feel, ten out of ten. Then I ask where on a ten point scale they might place themselves right now if ten is the best and zero is the worst they have ever felt. Usually clients will place themselves around a five because they are feeling calm and in control and have been talking with their worker for a while. We will then talk about a time when things could not have been any worse and we scale this as a zero. I will write this 'feelings thermometer' on one side of a piece of card.

Our next task, after talking about feelings and helping the client to understand the concept of scaling them, is to find the danger point. We might ask her at what point on that ten point scale she will start to think that she is losing control and needs to do something quickly. For some people it is a two, for others it could be a five. It is important to go with whatever number the client gives us because of course we are trying to get her to take charge. It is more important that the client begins making decisions than that she make the best possible one at this point. A client might say that she feels she is beginning to lose control when her feelings reach the level of seven. At that point we discuss the need to try something new rather than go down the same old path. 'It might not work the first time, but we need to keep on trying until it does'. We need to come up with some activities that she could do that would help her to change or control those bad feelings until they pass.

At this point we encourage the client to brainstorm and come up with as many ideas as they can about what they might do to break the chain of feelings which will lead to a crisis. I give them a few examples such as phone a friend or go for a walk. It does not matter how silly the ideas are as long as some of them are practical and useful. Usually people come up with ideas fairly quickly. It is important to validate all of the options as it is important that clients get the idea that they are capable of taking charge of their lives. We encourage clients to write down a few options and prioritise these. The one most likely to help is at the top of the list so that when they are needed, clients don't have to think about which to try first.

Workers usually do this on a piece of card, with the 'feelings thermometer' on one side and the options on the other. Sometimes it has been written inside an attractive greetings card or made into a fridge magnet.

In the example below, Jenny had lost her partner David, she would have suicidal thoughts sometimes and had a history of taking overdoses.

The front of the card is the 'feelings thermometer' ranging from best to worst and the 'trigger point' which in this instance is at number 4.

Jenny's crisis card . . . How am I feeling?

10   Malcolm was born, best thing that ever happened.
9   On Holiday with David – felt wonderful.
8   Feeling excited, something good, perhaps a party.
7   Exciting stuff to do like going out.
6   Feeling okay, stuff to do. Normal day.
5   Not really happy or unhappy. Not much Energy.
4   Thinking about David. Headache. Not crying.

TURN CARD OVER – TURN CARD OVER – TURN CARD OVER

3   Not good at all. Head pounding. Feeling angry.
2   Missing David – wishing I was with him.
1   When I took the pills because I couldn't take it anymore.

On the back of the card we have the alternative actions that the client can take when they notice that things are getting difficult.

Things to do when I am at 4

1 Call Cathy 02920 777 666   **6**   Stroke the cat

2 Call Joanne 01446 232426   **7**   Clean out the cupboard

3 Watch TV   **8**   Dye my hair green like I have always wanted to!

4 Listen to CDs   **9**   Read a magazine

5 Take a walk round the block   **10** Call my worker

The very act of devising such a card is empowering for the client, they are making decisions that will help them to take control of their emotions, they are accepting that they have choices, they are developing an understanding that a crisis is a thing that has a starting point, then develops into a full blown crisis and that they have choices all along the way. Once people understand that they can chose to divert away from the undesired emotional state, then they have to accept personal responsibility for their choices.

'I' messages

Very often families want to learn new communication skills. One of the most helpful things families can learn is 'I' messages. This is a way of keeping a situation calm and sending messages that influence another's behaviour. For instance a parent may use these messages to calm a child and make clear what behaviour they expect, an adult may be taught to use it with a partner and a worker may wish to use 'I' messages with a client.

A worker may use it with a family when they are finding it difficult to be heard:

I would really like to hear each point of view, and it is difficult for me to focus on you all at the same time.

People can learn to use messages in conflict situations. Often people will be saying 'you did this . . .' or 'he said that . . .' Sentences will be starting with the word 'You'. The strategy is to change direction and talk about yourself and not about the other person. These messages do not accuse or make the other person feel defensive but they do mean that the other person understands exactly what you want changed, their desire to co-operate is maximised, their self-esteem is maintained and so the relationship is maintained.

A worker may wish to practice doing this with a family or individual.

'I' messages start with the word 'I'. You want the other person to listen and understand you. People are more willing to listen if we talk about our own behaviour and feelings first. For example, instead of saying:

You never listen to what I say.

You might say:

I feel frustrated when you start talking before I'm finished.

'I' messages include:

- What happened (a specific behaviour that was seen or heard)
- How you feel about it
- Why you feel that way
- What you would like to be different

Here is how an 'I' message can be put together

I felt . . . (your feeling) when . . . (what happened), because . . . (why you feel that way, if you know). I would rather that you . . . (what you would like to be different).

I felt sad when you didn't take Billy to the park after you said you would, because Billy looked so sad. I would like it if next time you did what you told him you would do.

You are more likely to be able to discuss this and avoid an argument by saying it this way than by saying:

You ?!@#'! You always break your promises to Billy!

What can help:

1   Describing the behaviour based on observations, for example, talking about missing appointments instead of labelling people as irresponsible.

2   Using behavioural descriptions, not judgements, for example, yelling, not being an unfit parent.

3   Using gradations, not **all** or **none**, for example, 'You sometimes interrupt me,' instead of, 'You never listen.'

4   Speaking in the 'here and now', not 'there and then' for example, 'I want to talk,' instead of, 'You never listen.'

5   Sharing ideas, not giving advice, for example, 'I would like it if things would be different,' instead of 'You should shape up.'

6   Thinking about what is of value in this situation right now and what do I want to happen instead of getting everything off my chest in one go.

7   Providing only the amount of information that can be used, not what can be sent: do not overload.

Handout 1

Self-defeating and self-enhancing ideas

We all do it. Self talk can bring you up or send you down. The messages you give yourself, day by day, hour after hour, minute by minute have a real effect on how you feel about yourself, how you feel about others and how you behave.

Self-defeating ideas are often unrealistic thoughts put there in our childhood when people more powerful than ourselves told us stuff that made us feel useless. Some of them are left over from watching television, reading magazines or comparing ourselves to other people and comparing our lives with their lives. Sometimes self-defeating ideas come because perhaps we failed at something once and then always avoided doing that thing again and so never learned to succeed. Each time we had an opportunity to do it again, we told ourselves that we couldn't do that thing and reinforced the feeling of failure. Whatever the reason, I feel that self-defeating ideas are very harmful, I think of them as personal pollution that harms you and those that you love.

Self-defeating ideas create unhelpful or negative self-talk and this can be a vital factor in anger and depression. I often like to use the results of the strength and value cards to develop positive affirmations that people can use to replace negative self talk. When a client talks of feeling 'worthless' I can make an independent, factual and observed statement about the strongest thing I can find about them, 'you care about people very deeply and they seem to appreciate that' and so I try to 'hook' that idea onto the back of the feelings of worthlessness so that when they occur, people will remember the positive affirmation. A core aspect of this intervention is changing negative self talk into positive self talk. You will often do this with clients through solution focussed work and reflective listening:

> *I am useless*
>> *What is it about you that is useless?*
> *I just can't deal with David right now.*
>> *How bad is it on a scale of one to ten when one is the worst it has ever been and ten is the best?*
> *Three*
>> *So what are you doing that is stopping it from being a two or a one?*
> *I am not getting involved in his tantrums.*
>> *You are not getting involved.*
> *Yes I just stay out of the way until he calms down.*
>> *Is that useful?*

or:

> *Are you completely and utterly useless at everything?*
>> *No of course not.*
> *So what are you good at?*

Below are some thoughts about self-defeating ideas which can be left with the family and used as homework.

Self-defeating ideas	Self-enhancing ideas
I have to be loved or approved of by everyone.	There's no evidence I **need** approval or love. I have very few needs, the rest are wants. I can't always be loveable, and I can't be pleased all the time.
Certain things I do are bad or wicked and I should be blamed and punished.	Nobody is perfect. We all do things, but we're not bad people. Blaming and punishment are not the best way to change behaviour.
It is awful and horrible when things are not going the way I would like them to.	I've actually survived a lot. Awful is only a label I put on things.
Human unhappiness is externally caused and I have little or no ability to control my feelings about it.	I create my own feelings, and others have different feelings than me. No one else can make me feel good or bad.
If something is dangerous or fearsome, I must worry and be upset by it.	Worrying won't change anything. The more I worry, the less I do to solve things.
It is easier to avoid life's difficulties and responsibilities rather than face them.	If I try to take the easy way out, it may make things worse later. I can stand difficulties I just don't like them.
I need something or someone stronger than myself on whom to rely on.	I'm not a child and I can make it on my own. I can and do make good decisions.
I should be thoroughly competent, adequate and achieving in all aspects.	Nobody is perfect. I can make some mistakes and learn from them.
My past history determines my present behaviour, because once something strongly affected my life, it must do so forever.	I can change even the strongest habit. It is me, today, that determines what I believe and how I can make things better.
I should have certain and perfect control over things and people, including myself. There is a right, precise and perfect solution to human problems.	I cannot control others, especially how they think and feel. I don't need total control. There are usually several solutions to a problem. I can practice lots of solutions to find a good, not perfect, outcome.
I should become upset over other people's problems.	Being upset cannot change things. There are better ways to show concern.

Handout 2

Write down your own ideas that you feel affect the way you behave.

Thoughts I have that drag me down	Thoughts that lift me up
(Example – I can never get anything right)	(Example – I often get things right, I make a great lasagne and people like me)
(Example – nobody will ever love me because I am too fat)	(Example – Big men can look very sexy and powerful anyway if my weight was a problem to a woman then I wouldn't be interested in such a shallow person)

Handout 2

Anger management

The way we think can increase or decrease anger. Think about a time when you got angry and write about it on this sheet. What can you learn about getting angry and staying calm?

What happened?

Write about the event when you got angry

Bad News	Good News
Unhelpful things that you said to yourself	What could you have said to yourself instead?
Consequences of unhelpful things that you said to yourself (Feelings)	Consequences of helpful things that you said to yourself (Less intense feelings)
Your behaviour after you said the unhelpful things to yourself	Your behaviour after you said the helpful things to yourself

Handout 4

Six steps to anger

When you get angry you go through different steps, do these feel familiar to you?

Step 1. I want something, or I don't want something.
Step 2. I don't get what I want.
Step 3. I begin to 'awfulise' and think things like:

- It's terrible that this has happened.

- I must stop this.

- I can't stand this.

- This isn't fair.

Step 4. I move the focus to the other person and change my wants to demands.

- He shouldn't do this to me

- Who does he think he is?

- I'm not going to let her get away with this

- She can't do this to me

Starting to get mad now!

Step 5. I equate the other person with his behaviour; I begin to judge and blame.

- He's a $*?@# for doing this to me.

- She's a rotten friend, and after all I've done for her.

Step 6. I reach the point of no return. The other person must now be punished.

- Bad people ought to be punished.

- She needs to be taken down off her high horse.

- He needs to learn a lesson.

I know these feelings so well, I used to have a real problem with anger but looking at this now makes me smile and wince at the same time. It is one thing being able to identify the stages, but a completely different thing knowing what to do about it. Sometimes the stages happen so fast it is like being on a train with no stopping point to get off.

The way out is to realise that you are getting on the train in the first place, you need a plan, answer the questions on the next page to create your plan.

Handout 5

Five step anger management plan

1 I know I'm getting angry because . . .

Describe feelings, thoughts and behaviour

2 What I want is . . .

Ideas: How do you want to behave? What do you want to think about yourself? What positive thoughts should you be having? . . .

3 What I want to avoid is . . .

4 My plan is . . .

Ideas: To take five deep breaths before I open my mouth or . . .

5 My back up plan is . . .

What do you do if plan 'a' doesn't work?

Handout 6

Tick the thoughts you might use.

Include them in your personal safety plan.

Can you think of any more?

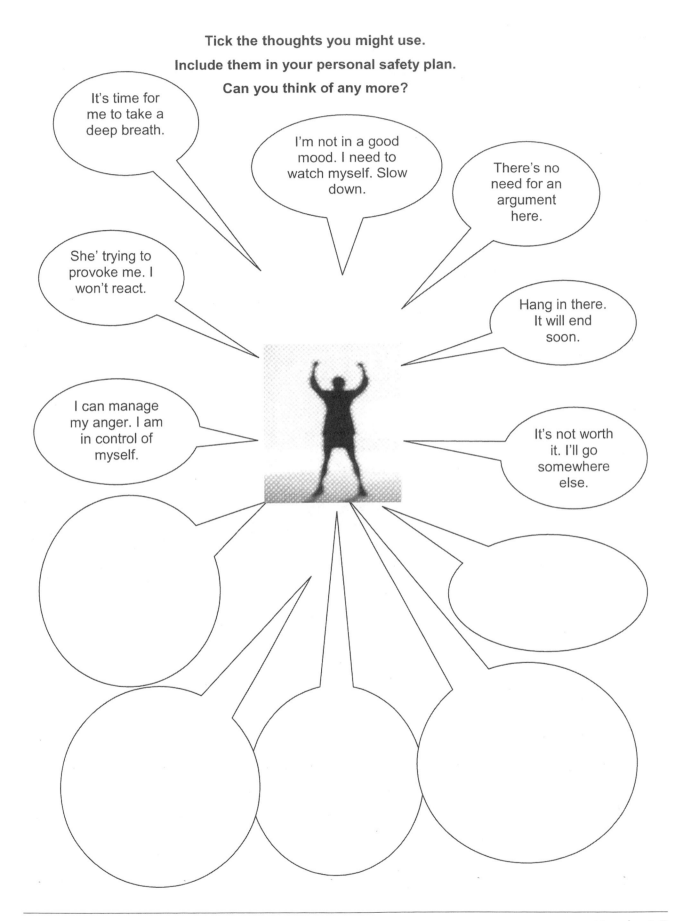

It's time for me to take a deep breath.

I'm not in a good mood. I need to watch myself. Slow down.

There's no need for an argument here.

She' trying to provoke me. I won't react.

Hang in there. It will end soon.

I can manage my anger. I am in control of myself.

It's not worth it. I'll go somewhere else.

Cognitive distortions

All or nothing thinking: You see things in black and white categories. If your performance falls short of perfect, you see yourself as a total failure.

Over generalisation: You see a single negative event as a never-ending pattern of defeat.

Mental filter: You take the negative details and magnify them while filtering out all positive aspects of a situation.

Minimising: You reject positive experiences by insisting they 'don't count' for some reason or other. In this way you can maintain a negative belief that is contradicted by your everyday experiences.

Mind reading: You arbitrarily conclude that someone is reacting negatively to you and you don't bother to check it out.

Fortune telling: You anticipate that things will turn out badly and you feel convinced that your prediction is an already established fact.

Catastrophising: You exaggerate the importance of things, such as your goof-up or someone else's achievement.

'Should' statements: You have a list of ironclad rules about how you and other people should act. You feel guilty if you break the rules and angry if anybody else does. 'Should' statements often come from things you were told as a child – are they always sensible?

Emotional reasoning: You assume that negative emotions necessarily reflect the way things are. 'I feel bad, so I must be bad'.

Labelling: Instead of describing your error, you attach a negative label to yourself: 'I'm a loser'.

Personalisation: You think everything people do or say is some kind of reaction to you.

Entitlement: You believe that there are things you rightfully deserve just for being who you are, regardless of whether you have earned them.

Handout 8

An action plan to help parents manage children's behaviour

The deepest principle in human nature is the craving to be appreciated.

William James, Psychologist (1842–1910)

1   If there is a problem with your child's behaviour, **STOP**, think about it and make sure it really is a problem before you do or say anything. It might be a 'should' statement left over from your childhood that isn't relevant any more. We all have 'should' statements: 'children *should* be seen and not heard', 'girls *should* be clean', 'shoes *should* be put away tidily'. All bits of teaching left over that may not be important any more. Why destroy the peace if it is not really a problem? On the other hand you may be over-reacting because you are stressed. If it really matters, then five minutes cooling off period won't do any harm.

2   If you decide that it is a problem. Decide what you want to happen. Ask yourself if it is realistic, can you make it happen? Is it important enough? If you feel that you cannot make it happen, why try? That will only teach the child that he can get away with it. Just say 'It makes me feel unhappy when you do that' then ignore them while they carry on.

3   When you have decided what it is you want to happen, say it aloud to your children as clearly as possible. 'I want you to put your night things on and brush your teeth please.'

4   When they ignore you, or argue, or answer back, take no notice of their bad behaviour. Just repeat what it is that you want to happen. Over and over again if necessary, **do not say anything else at all.**

5   Pay no attention to the bad behaviour. Do not argue, do not shout, do not make eye contact, do not talk to them apart from saying what it is that you want. Do not reward bad behaviour, even by paying attention to it. If a child is behaving badly to get your attention, then ignore it. Do not teach them that bad behaviour is a good way of getting attention. Do not talk about bad behaviour after it is over.

6   Continue to ignore bad behaviour if you can. Make sure that you can make everybody safe, either by removing the people in danger, or removing dangerous objects. Do not speak to him until he calms down.

7   Be a good example. Children learn how to behave by watching their parents. If you scream, shout and swear, they will learn to scream, shout and swear.

8   Pay lots and lots of attention when a child is being good. Show them that good behaviour is a great way of getting the attention they want. You can do the washing up later, play with the kids. Give one to one attention when the child is being good.

9   Give positive comments and attention at least three times as often as you give negative attention or tell the child off. Work hard at remembering to praise your child when s/he is good. This leads them into being good more often. Say things like:
   - *I like it when you play nicely like that.*
   - *It makes me happy when you help me by putting your things away.*
   - *It's great when we get on well together like this isn't it.*
   - *Thanks for keeping yourself busy just now while I was getting on with the cooking.*

See how these comments use what are called 'I' messages. When you talk about your feelings it is very powerful. If you find this useful, talk to your worker about other kinds of 'I' messages that help you to get your message across without arguing or anybody getting upset, ask them for handouts one and ten in this set.

Handout 9

92 Ways to say 'very good'

1 You're on the right track now!
2 You're doing a great job!
3 You did a lot of work today!
4 Now you've figured it out.
5 That's RIGHT!!
6 That's the way.
7 You're really going to town.
8 You're doing fine.
9 Now you have it.
10 Nice going.
11 That's coming along nicely.
12 That's great.
13 You did it that time.
14 GREAT!!!
15 FANTASTIC!!!
16 TERRIFIC!!!
17 Good for you!
18 You outdid yourself today.
19 GOOD WORK.
20 That's better.
21 EXCELLENT.
22 That's a good (boy/girl).
23 Good job (name).
24 That's the best you have ever done.
25 Good going.
26 Keep it up.
27 That's really nice.
28 WOW!
29 Keep up the good work.
30 Much better.
31 That's very much better!
32 Good thinking!
33 SUPER!
34 Exactly right.
35 You make it look easy.
36 I've never seen anyone do it better.
37 You are doing that much better today.
38 Way to go!!
39 Not bad!
40 Superb.
41 You're getting better every day.
42 WONDERFUL!
43 I knew you could do it.
44 Keep working on it, you're getting better.
45 You're doing really beautifully.
46 You're really working hard today.
47 That's the way to do it!
48 THAT'S IT!
49 Nothing can stop you now.
50 You've got it made.
51 You're very good at that.
52 Now you have the hang of it!
53 I'm very proud of you.
54 You certainly did well today.
55 You've just about got it.
56 That's good.
57 I'm happy to see you working.
58 I'm proud of the way you worked.
59 That's the right way to do it.
60 You are really learning a lot.
61 That's better than ever.
62 That's quite an improvement.
63 That kind of work makes me happy!
64 MARVELLOUS!
65 Now you've figured it out.
66 PERFECT!
67 That's not half bad.
68 FINE!!
69 You've got your brain in gear today.
70 You figured that out fast.
71 You remembered.
72 You're really improving.
73 I think you've got it.
74 Well look at you.
75 You've got that down.
76 TREMENDOUS!
77 OUTSTANDING!
78 I like that.
79 Couldn't have done it better myself.
80 Now that's what I call a fine job.
81 You did that very well.
82 Congratulations.
83 That was first class work.
84 Right on!
85 Sensational.
86 That's the best ever.
87 Good remembering!
88 You haven't missed a thing.
89 It's a pleasure to teach you work.
90 You really make my job fun.
91 One more time and you'll have it.
92 You must have been practicing!

Handout 10

Tips for coping with depression

1   Don't try to solve all of life's problems in a day.

2   Keep your mind and body active.

3   Resolve each and every day to do something that you have avoided doing.

4   Try to be agreeable to others.

5   Do not criticise or blame others.

6   Dress as nicely as possible, this will help you regain your self esteem.

7   Try to do something to help somebody else.

8   Share your problems with a friend but don't expect them to provide solutions.

9   Have courage to change what can be changed, but accept what cannot be changed.

10   Try to develop a positive attitude to negative life events.

I found these ten tips in my office when I moved in. I have no idea where they came from. If you wrote them, please accept my apologies for stealing them, perhaps you will enjoy the fact that more people are getting the benefit of them.

Handout 11

Tips for coping with stress

1 Avoid self medication with nicotine, too much alcohol, coffee or other drugs.

2 Work off stress. Physical activity is a terrific outlet.

3 Don't put off relaxing. Use a relaxation technique every day.

4 Get enough sleep and rest to recharge your batteries.

5 If you become sick, don't try to carry on as if you are not.

6 Agree with somebody. Life should not be a constant battleground.

7 Learn to accept what you cannot change.

8 Manage your time better and delegate.

9 Know when you are tired and do something about it.

10 Plan ahead by saying 'no' now. You may prevent too much pressure piling up in the future.

I found these ten tips in my office when I moved in. I have no idea where they came from. If you wrote them, please accept my apologies for stealing them, perhaps you will enjoy the fact that more people are getting the benefit of them.

Handout 12

Tips for coping with panic

1   Your feelings are only normal responses by your body and mind which have become exaggerated.

2   These feelings are not harmful and will fade in time.

3   Become aware of what is happening in your body now and stay focussed in the present moment. Begin to slow down your breathing.

4   Continue to breathe more slowly for some time. Relax, letting go some of the tension held in your body.

5   Do not anticipate future events, stay focussed on what is happening now.

6   Do not fight against the feelings, but accept them, allowing them to flow through you. This helps them to fade away more quickly.

7   Try to measure your level of anxiety noticing when the level begins to fall.

8   Stay focussed on breathing more slowly and deliberately. Releasing the tension, from shoulders, face, stomach, arms and legs. Each time you breathe out allow yourself to relax a little more.

9   Re-read these notes slowly, several times if necessary.

10   Begin to return to what you were doing, but take your time.

I found these ten tips in my office when I moved in. I have no idea where they came from. If you wrote them, please accept my apologies for stealing them, perhaps you will enjoy the fact that more people are getting the benefit of them.

Handout 13

Learn how to relax

Many years ago I taught relaxation and self hypnosis classes and I had a lot of students who suffered from a variety of problems with anxiety and stress. Relaxation can help you to get back in control of your own body when you are feeling anxious, stressed, angry, tense or focussed on the 'wrong' things. When you get angry or anxious, you start by thinking in a certain way which makes your body release chemicals that make you act in a certain way. For example anger is often brought on by thinking that you have been 'wronged' in some way, your muscles start to tense and your body releases adrenaline which makes you feel even more angry.

Anxiety can be brought on by encountering a situation which makes you afraid, this releases chemicals which make your heart beat faster and this makes you more anxious.

The most important way of taking control is to talk with your therapist about any negative automatic thoughts that might make you feel anxious, stressed or angry. Many of those thoughts are based on false rules and ideas that you have learned, ask for handout number five.

Another thing you can do is teach your body to behave in a more calm way.

If you do the exercises regularly and take them seriously, you are learning to take control of your body. Your body may fight back from time to time and make you feel that you couldn't be bothered or that the exercises do not help. They do help.

Don't expect to be able to achieve total relaxation straight away. You may still feel a little tense during the session. It takes time and daily practice. But when you have achieved real relaxation you will know. You will feel warm and comfortable, almost as if you are floating, and this is a very pleasant sensation. You are learning a skill which you will be able to use anywhere, with practice you will be able to relax whenever you have to face a difficult situation.

How to do it

1 Find a warm quiet place where you will not be disturbed. Lie on a bed or better still, sit in a good chair with your head supported. Play quiet music if you like. Try to relax for a moment or two. Either close your eyes or fix them on an object or mark on the wall.

2 Breathe in slowly through your nose, making your stomach rise. Breathe out through your mouth. Think of the word 'CALM' each time you breathe out.

3 Begin by tightening your **right fist**. Tighten it up. Hold it tight for a few seconds. Now relax it suddenly. Feel the relaxation come into your arm, right up to your shoulder. Like a feeling of warmth passing up your arm. Notice and enjoy that feeling of relaxation.

4 Now go to your **left hand**. Make a fist and tighten it up. Hold it for a few seconds and then relax it suddenly. Feel and enjoy the feeling of relaxation in your arm and shoulder. Slow your breathing and let your whole body relax.

5 Now pull your **shoulders** up and hold them for a few seconds. Suddenly relax them, letting your shoulders and arms hang loose. Feel the relaxation coming into your shoulders

and neck. Enjoy that feeling, slow your breathing and continue to breathe slowly and deeply letting your whole body relax.

6   Move on to your **neck**. It is often your neck which is most stiff and tense and may be the most difficult part to relax. Push your neck back and hold it there. Tighten your neck muscles and hold them tight for a moment. Now relax them suddenly and enjoy that feeling of relaxation.

7   Next tighten up your **face** muscles. Make a frown. Clench your teeth tightly and wrinkle your forehead. Hold for a moment then quickly relax the muscles and slow your breathing. Enjoy the sensation of relaxation in your face and through your body.

8   Move on to your **stomach**. Pull in your tummy and make yourself as slim as possible. Hold that position for a moment and then quickly relax, slowing your breathing. Just let your whole body loosen up and relax and slow your breathing right down.

9   When you are comfortable arch your **back** and tighten your back muscles. Hold for a moment and relax quickly and feel the relaxation spreading through your body.

10.   When you are comfortable, Push the toes of both feet away from you and stretch your **legs**, tightening up the muscles. Suddenly relax your legs and enjoy the feeling of relaxation. Slow your breathing right down and let your body go loose.

11   Stay where you are, continue to slow your breathing right down. Think warm relaxing thoughts, a warm beach or luxurious bed. Think, 'Relax', 'Calm', 'Slow down', 'Take it easy'.

12   When you feel you have done enough, count down, 'three, two, one, wake up'. Now you are back in the real world.

Remember

If you have problems with anxiety, anger or stress, your body may have learned to be automatically tense in some situations. This tension in your body makes you afraid, angry or worried (of what may happen, of what people will think) and this heightened emotion triggers the release of adrenaline and it is this chemical that makes you tearful, feel sick, shake, have swallowing difficulty, dizziness, palpitations, more tension. You can't relax because you can't turn off the adrenaline.

Your body can learn to relax instead, but you have to teach it. You teach it by practising. Make sure that you give your body good feelings so that it learns there is no need to be tense. Try to concentrate and stay awake, you don't learn much if you fall asleep.

Visualisation

When you are able to relax, you may want to take things a step further. Did you do a card game with your worker where you talked about some of the positive and good things about you, your strengths and values? At another time did you talk about what life would be like if there was a miracle? Think about those things and come up with an image of how you would like things to be; less angry, calmer, more relaxed, nicer home, new decoration, better relationships with your children. Pick a nice positive image before you start to relax and then fantasise about this while you are deeply relaxed. Imagine it as if it were real today. Visualise yourself being happy, coping well, experiencing happy relationships with the people you care about.

When you do this you teach your mind to think more positively and make it more likely that these things can be real. If negative thinking makes bad things happen, which it clearly does, then why shouldn't positive thinking make positive things more likely to happen?

Handout 14

CHAPTER 10

Working With Suicidal Clients

We sometimes find ourselves working with clients who are suicidal. Our general policy is to take suicidal threats or gestures very seriously. Even if we, or others, think the client doesn't intend to follow through, we advise intervening. It is important for the client to get the message that:

- Someone cares a lot.

- When you talk suicide there will be a consequence.

Some of these consequences might be:

- We refuse to let the client be alone.

- We tell others in the family.

- We may call mental health services to evaluate for possible commitment.

- We take the client to hospital.

Is the client suicidal?

Almost every person experiences suicidal thoughts at one time or another. Sometimes these feelings are fleeting, other times more intense and appealing. Some people have habitually considered suicide for many years.

The client may give indirect or direct clues that she is considering suicide:

- She may say things like: 'I can't handle this anymore.' 'The kids would be better off without me.'

- He may give away possessions, write a will, and tie up loose ends.

- She may tell others goodbye in indirect ways: 'You did all you could do.' 'Always remember that I love you, no matter what happens.'

- Sudden recovery from depression or anxiety can be a danger sign. The client may feel better because a decision to commit suicide has been made and he is no longer struggling with conflicted feelings.

- The client may make a clear statement: 'I'm going to kill myself.'

- There may be a suicide note: teenagers in particular may practice writing such a note.

- The client may have deliberately obtained the means for suicide by hoarding pills, keeping a knife in the bedroom.

- Sometimes things are done openly in preparation for death, such as disposing of personal items or saying goodbye to special people.

Be direct – 'Are you thinking of killing yourself?' (this is one time you **don't** want to reframe into more positive phrasing). An answer of 'no' doesn't necessarily mean that the client is not suicidal. It is possible for suicide ideation to be present even when there is not an immediate plan to die.

- How will you do it?

- When will you do it?

Don't accept 'I'll be fine', or 'I'm ok' – they could mean, 'I'll be fine as soon as I'm dead'. Or 'I'm ok because I've decided to remove myself from this pain'. Use 'I' messages if necessary, like 'I'm concerned that you may not be safe'.

Immediate risk is determined by

Availability of method – If the client plans to shoot himself, but has no gun, there is a lower risk. If the client says, 'maybe I'll just take all my pills' and has lots of pills, the risk is higher.

Lethality of method – Lower lethality increases the time you have in which to intervene. Starving oneself to death is low lethality, overdose on pills is higher, gunshot or hanging is highest.

- How specific are the details of the plan? The more specific the plan the higher the risk.

- If the suicidal person uses drugs and/or alcohol, the risk is higher, because these substances diminish impulse control.

- If the suicidal client is a teenager, they may tell you one thing and do something entirely different. This is because teens can be very impulsive and often experience dramatic mood swings, which alter the intentions with little or no warning. In such cases, be alert to other signals we have already discussed.

Some general thoughts on intervention

- Most people who are suicidal don't want to die. They are simply in a lot of pain, they want the pain to stop and feel hopeless or helpless to stop it with any tool other than death.

- Often suicidal feelings are situational and transient: if you can help the client get through the day, week, or month of intense suicidal feelings, they will often not be at such risk again.

- Most people who consider suicide are ambivalent: that's why they are letting you in on the secret. Remember to use that ambivalence to work with their 'survivor' side, the part that wants to stay alive (there must be one, or the client would be dead by now).

Strategies for intervention

- Stay calm. People need the same modelling around suicide that they need for the socially unacceptable feelings such as anger. We will be most helpful if we are a safe place for clients to work through their suicidal feelings.

- Remember that there are a lot of things you can do to help. If the client has an immediate plan or intent to kill themselves and if the means of suicide are present, ask the client to reduce the accessibility by giving the means to you or flushing pills down the toilet.

- It may be necessary to send or take a suicidal client to a hospital emergency room for assessment for psychiatric admission. Be aware that your client may have to wait several hours before being seen.

- Hospitalisation may not be available and may be an unpleasant experience.

- Check out previous history. 'Have you felt this way before?' 'What helped you get through it?'

- Set monitoring of client safety or client's suicidal feelings. The therapist, the supervisor, the client's friends or family, and the client themselves can do this monitoring.

- Teach a client how to use a feelings thermometer to assist with monitoring and a Crisis Card to trigger coping strategies.

- Reflective listening is essential because it may help relieve the tension of the client's feelings, but be alert to the point at which it is no longer helpful and they are ruminating.

- Get a 'no self-harm' contract – 24 hours, 2 days, whatever you can get. If the client won't contract about self-harm, see if you can get a contract for something the client will do **before** they hurt themselves (call you, call crisis line, etc.).

- Give your client a reason to hang on a little longer.
  Things will change.
  You won't always feel this way.
  Your kids won't understand – all they will know is that you abandoned them.

- A statement some workers like is 'You can kill yourself any time; try these other things first'.

- Confront the client about what they think will happen after their death (both to them and to the people in their lives). 'Who will discover the body?' 'How will everyone feel?' Don't romanticise – be realistic about blood, vomit, anger, feelings of betrayal and abandonment.

- Do whatever it takes to keep your client engaged and alive.

- If suicide is a response to a situational pressure, help alleviate the pressure, but don't remove them all. Some of the pressure is part of what is keeping the client alive. For example: a mother may be under lots of stress from her children but also chooses to keep going because of them.

Consultation

- Get peer and supervisor consultation ASAP and as often as you need. Be as aggressive as you need to be in getting consultation. Your supervisor won't know that you need more help unless you say so.

- Pay attention to your gut feelings and what it is telling you about the situation, what is going on, how much help you need, how successful the interventions are.

Therapist self-care

- Remember that suicide is an option – it is not a good one, and not one with which you agree, but it is a legitimate choice.

- You are responsible to do all you can to help, but the client holds the ultimate responsibility. Just as with parenting and anger management skills, we can teach but the client is the final determiner of whether or not the skills are used.

- It's hard to listen to suicidal thoughts and help a client cope, but better that than to not know how your client is feeling. It is better to be fired by a live client, or to have to handle a client's anger, than to have a dead client. So if you have to risk the therapeutic relationship in order to save your client's life, do it.

CHAPTER 11

Staff Care

It is a widespread belief that while it is virtuous to love others, it is sinful to love oneself . . . if it is a virtue to love my neighbour as a human being, it must be a virtue – not a vice – to love myself, since I am a human being too.

Erich Fromm, *The Art of Loving* (1957)

We have looked at a lot of strategies that you can use with your clients to make their lives better. You are an important part of that system, if you are not functioning well, then it would be foolish to assume that you can help your clients to function well. If you feel hopeless then that feeling will be transmitted to clients. You may be working very hard to make their lives better, but are you putting any effort into your own life?

This intervention can be very demanding of people working alone in the field, closely with families in crisis. While you are working with a family in their home, there are no resources you can draw on other than those that you have with you, whether they are physical, intellectual, emotional or spiritual.

Wendy

Wendy rang me at 11 pm, she had taken a deliberate overdose and rang me up 'to say goodbye'. I called an ambulance which she sent away. She had sent her children to her sisters for the evening so that she could die. So I visited. At six o'clock the next morning she was still alive and we were driving round the city in my car looking for cigarettes. In those seven hours I kept her awake, drinking coffee, smoking cigarettes, talking, looking for positives, accepting her grief and anger at the loss of a child who had died from meningitis. She survived and so did I. Sadly I saw Wendy only once after that. She moved away and I do not know what happened to her.

This is perhaps the most extreme experience in terms of work/life balance that I can remember in five years of doing this work, thankfully such events are very rare. I have the freedom and autonomy to manage my own working day so that I can take time to recuperate. This autonomy comes from the management structure which mirrors the service principles of trust and honesty, is confident in its ability to support staff in their work and which provides workers with the confidence and the emotional resources which enable them to do this demanding work.

Most of the time I work nine to five, or ten to six, or seven-thirty to three-thirty. Whatever fits in with what my clients need. I sometimes work a Saturday morning and take Monday morning off. I rarely work more that 38 hours a week and when I do I either save the extra hours up for a few days extra holiday or stay in bed in the morning, miss all the traffic and spend time with my children.

This section holds some ideas that can help you to make decisions and help you to feel safe. The first one of these is our safety policy.

Safety policy

Staying safe and keeping your colleague safe:

- Contract with another team member to look after each other and provide a safety service. Ideally teams are set up in pairs.

- When you take on a new family, inform your buddy of their name, address and telephone number and any concerns you have about safety. Buddy needs to know where you are.

- Remember to ask your buddy for the details of their clients and record this somewhere you will be able to access when out of hours.

- Sign off with your buddy each day.

- Agree a time by which you will talk.

If you are called out at night or at the weekend

1 Inform your buddy or partner/manager/other.

2 Inform Emergency Duty Team (EDT).
   – Tell them the address of where you are visiting.
   – Give your Vehicle description and registration details.

If your buddy does not sign off with you by the agreed time:

1 Call them on their mobile and at home.

2 If you get no response call your manager; then inform EDT giving above information.

3 Call the police.

113

Mobile and home numbers and vehicle details

Name	Mobile phone	Home phone	Vehicle description	Vehicle registration

Guidelines for contacting your supervisor

Immediately

- Anytime, 24 hours a day, 7 days a week, when the worker becomes aware of any concern for the safety of any family member or themselves. If the supervisor is unavailable, they must call other agency staff.

- Any case with the clients presenting serious threats to self or others should be discussed daily with supervisor during periods of instability.

At the next opportunity

This means do not wait for group consultation or regularly scheduled meetings.

- You're having trouble getting people to meet with you, for intake or during the intervention.

- Any time a family fires you or avoids seeing you.

- Any time you are lying awake because you're worried about a case or yourself.

- Any time you are feeling pressured to make a decision immediately and feel a better decision could be made with help.

- You are having difficulty ending your intervention with the family.

Seek individual supervision when

- You are having difficulty defusing clients.

- You are having difficulty formulating goals after the first week.

- You don't like the family or individual in the family.

- No progress is made on goals.

- You think the family would be better off apart.

- You're putting in lots of overtime.

- You feel overwhelmed, tired, depressed, panicky.

Potentially difficult issues

Helpful thoughts about being called out

- It will really mean to lot to them if I come through now.

- They will probably be upset if they are calling now . . . if I listen, I'll learn lots.

- I can really help people at times like this.

- If this is not a 'crisis' I can be assertive and/or set limits. (Being careful not to cut off a client prematurely, but rather structuring the call.)

- This doesn't have to take all evening.

- If this gets too much, I can always call my supervisor.

- I'd rather take care of things now rather than let them build up.

- I can be a real person with them and let them know what's happening with me.

- This gives me a chance to start working on things . . . a head start for tomorrow.

- I can remind them to use/practice their new skills.

- I can tell them if I'm worn out or pressed for time. (Be sure clients know back-up numbers to call).

- This might be time to do some real problem solving.

- If this gets to be too much, I can arrange to call them instead, when it's more convenient for me.

- I'll be free tomorrow morning to do something I want.

- It's great to sleep in.

- This makes me different, which I like.

- I like not working 9 to 5.

- Remember why they call it the 9 to 5 drag – this job isn't a drag, it's not boring.

- Often I stay out of traffic jams.

- This enables me to take time off for boring things (e.g. hair cuts, bank, childrens' social activities).

- The queues to do things are shorter in the week.

- I have a wonderful, flexible job.

- I remind myself of the times I had to be at work by 9 and the regimented schedule.

■ Many other people have more difficult schedules than this (e.g. airline staff, railway staff etc.)

■ I care about these families. If they're really hurting, I want to be there.

■ I don't get called often.

■ Maybe I can really make a difference.

When progress is slow

■ My objective is not to take them to their destination, but just to put them back on track.

■ Not all families are going to accomplish as much as others.

■ I did the best I could, so did they.

■ You can't win them all.

■ Any progress we made is better than none at all.

■ Part of it might be a societal problem . . . not enough services.

■ Sometimes the most I can do with a family is to give them a positive experience of social work.

■ I can only do so much, keep focussed.

■ The family is doing the best they can with the skills they have.

■ I don't know at the time of termination exactly how much good has been done.

■ Maybe my expectations are too high – maybe the family has learned something they will use at a later date.

■ Maybe it wasn't a teachable moment for the family.

■ I have presented a lot of information. I have planted a seed. They might use this information in the future.

Ideas for structuring the worker's time

■ Schedule a week's worth of appointments at once, or as many as possible.

■ Set limits on sessions when appropriate.

■ Educate clients what is appropriate to call you for. Time limit non-crisis phone calls rather than talking for an undetermined amount of time. Give examples of when a call would be appropriate (according to the situation).

■ Plan to take one weekend per month off, i.e. go out of town or be unavailable to clients. (Be sure to arrange back up).

■ Plan ways to do something for yourself every day.

- Alert your social support network to call you often for support – assign different people different days to do this.

- Brainstorm and practice ways to say NO to clients who are using up your time inappropriately.

- Turn on the VCR and record the show I was watching.

- Get an answering machine to screen the calls for what needs immediate attention.

- Educate my clients as to what might be appropriate times to call, especially for non-emergency situations.

- Structure family interactions/time/activities between visits to avoid unnecessary conflict requiring therapist's intervention.

- If I'm really tired, unplug phone. (If this is done, back up arrangements must be made).

- Make sure my clients have back up numbers (supervisor and colleague).

- Monitor/chart how many phone calls are received to get an accurate picture, often the times they occur is less than perceived. If it is happening frequently, consult with supervisor.

- If feeling preoccupied afterwards, go for a walk, watch TV, read etc.

- Talk with my supervisor about it.

- Call my client ahead of time (before I leave).

- Make sure I schedule time off during the day to shop, go the movies, etc.

- Try to work weekends so kids can be with their Dad/Mum instead of a sitter.

- Don't over-commit myself to too many long days in a row. (Sometimes this can't be helped, but possibly I could arrange other coverage if this is overwhelming).

- Make early evening appointments so that I am not out too late.

- Grumble/complain and then let go.

- When scheduling regular appointments, try to find a mutually agreeable time.

- Plan something fun each day.

- Structure free time; have fun things to do.

- Schedule early Saturday morning or Sunday evening so you have the rest of the weekend off.

- If something I need/want to do is important, I ask for coverage.

- Be tentative with friends so it's not so unexpected if I have to cancel.

- Re-schedule plans.

- If I start feeling like a martyr, I consult with my supervisor.

- Improve giving families skills/support so it doesn't happen so often.

- Set reasonable limits . . . don't cancel my plans when there is really no reason.

- Take TOIL/annual leave. (Be sure to arrange coverage).

- Ask my friends/family to be supportive in doing this job.

- Pamper myself afterwards.

- Occasionally cancel/re-arrange appointments with my family.

Not accomplishing as much as you'd like

- Re-evaluate if goals were reasonable.

- Look more closely at what clients say.

- Review what we did get done . . . step towards goal . . . what did and didn't work.

- Remind myself of people's right to change how and when they want.

- Drop unrealistic goals.

- Use your colleagues for feedback on number of goals, etc.

- Read client evaluation follow-ups.

- Scale goal weekly to measure even small amounts of change/progress.

- Have more confidence in community resources. Refer families for ongoing help.

- Go back to referral and review changes that have occurred since.

- Talk to my supervisor and team.

- Change the goal.

- Attempt to have family members engage in behavioural rehearsals by setting it up as an experiment – keep track of what happens when the parent uses alternative behaviours.

- Self-disclosure regarding lack of progress on a goal. Check out the family members' perception to see if they feel there has been progress.

- When presenting a new intervention, ask the family what they think of your idea.

- It is sometimes helpful to write a pros and cons list of each option when it appears as if there is an impasse.

- Have the parent reinforce themselves for attempts at behaviour change.

- Look at old follow-ups. Remind yourself to keep this family in perspective. Look back at past cases where you felt more successful.

- Get support from other people, get ideas from others and carry out a literature review.

- Reinforce yourself for your efforts.

- Re-define the meaning of success; sometimes success is defined as 'I did not get fired by the family'.

Our workers

We often use the term 'therapist' to describe our workers trained in this model, although 'therapist' is an uncomfortable term for many, we use it because our workers come from a variety of disciplines. Clients routinely call us 'therapists', 'counsellors', 'support workers' and 'social workers'. Good social work practice is informed by knowledge, understanding and skills in psychology, social work and counselling. Our workers have professional backgrounds in each of those fields. Their qualifications have included Counselling Diplomas, DipSW, to PhD. We look for very experienced workers who are at the peak of their practice, our aim is to keep good workers operational and so we pay salaries at a rate which gives them a choice of remaining operational rather than move into team management. We train our own therapists and we train therapists from other local authorities at training events we hold once or twice a year.

We work in buddy teams of two workers who have responsibility for looking after each other. We do not visit together or share cases in any way apart from providing peer supervision for each other. Workers need to have access to a supervisor and we believe that supervisors should be people who have experience of using the intervention.

CHAPTER 12

Real People

Learning to live is learning to let go.

Sogyal Rinpoche, Tibetan Buddhist Teacher

To accomplish great things, we must not only act, but also dream; not only plan, but also believe.

Anatole France

Here, right at the end, I wanted to introduce you to some real people. In one sense it does not seem right somehow that they do not appear until the end. When thinking about my work, the clients are not my last thoughts but my first. However, I wanted you to end this book with real people on your mind.

I hope that earlier in the manual I have been able to give you a taste of how particular intervention styles or tools can work with individuals. Most of those extracts of dialogue are drawn from my memories of working with particular people. Here their stories although brief are more complete. Of course some information has been changed to protect the confidentiality of the individuals and families concerned, however the essential information is accurate.

Tina

Tina had two young children, baby Michael and five year old Martin. Martin was unruly and difficult to control. Tina had been a heroin user but with the help of a residential rehab she had stopped some years ago. She had some serious medical problems related to a lifetime of drug misuse and prostitution and physical and sexual abuse, and she was prescribed painkillers and anti-depressants. Her GP cut her medication drastically and when Tina began to withdraw from it, she found she was not able to cope. She protested aggressively and was struck off her GP's list.

I became involved when the childcare team were considering removing Tina's children because she was withdrawing and was unable to cope with them. I worked with Tina to help her to focus on the most pressing issues, we worked together to get a new GP and after a few difficult but increasingly focussed days Tina was back on medication with a new GP and had a clear and agreed plan for reduction.

By the end of our four weeks together, Tina had explored the feelings behind Martin's behaviour and as a result had started a new regime which addressed his feelings of insecurity by using a behavioural approach which provided clear and appropriate boundaries and consequences for good and misbehaviour. His behaviour improved radically. Tina had worked on her communication skills so that she was able to be assertive with professionals without becoming emotional and she had begun to use her new negotiating skills to manage her difficult relationship with her parents and siblings.

Shortly afterward the case was closed to children's services. I continue to see Tina on rare occasions, we speak at Christmas, she now has a new partner, a new child, the life she wanted and is writing a book about her experiences.

Tina set five clear goals:

1   To register with a new GP and become stable on medication.

2   To set clear routines for her son, focussing on making his bedroom an attractive place for him, having a clear bed time and a time to get up for school.

3   To move to a more suitable property.

4   Setting clear boundaries so that other people around her are clear what they can and cannot 'get away with'.

5   Having access to a counsellor who meets her needs.

Tina achieved three of her goals during her four week intervention and achieved the other two in the weeks following the intervention.

> *The dedicated time and effort of the worker has put right many of the problems . . . I am less dependant on others . . . without this, my problem would have seriously deteriorated . . . I have a balanced approach to my responsibilities . . . I have achieved so much.*
>
> Tina in a letter to the service

Sue and Lee

Sue and Lee had a baby – Rose. Both parents were drinking heavily and there had been related incidents of domestic violence. The baby was not being presented for medical appointments and the childcare team were considering removing her.

Our work together focussed on what the family wanted for the future. Both parents said that they wanted what they called a 'normal family life'. We discussed what this meant for them and they said that they wanted to live without drink or violence or the threat of the family being broken up. Both parents had a deep distrust of social services and showed many of the behaviours consistent with resistance. We worked first of all on reframing the childcare professionals concerns so that Sue and Lee began to understand that the childcare team's aims for a safe childhood coincided with their own. We explored what they needed to do to make the threat of removal go away. We helped the family to organise appointments, we planned safe and sensible drinking levels and worked intensively on communication skills so that the threat of violence was minimised.

During the four weeks both parents became clear about their aims as parents, Rose continues to attend all of her appointments, they learned assertiveness skills and 'I' messages, Lee started to attend a domestic violence project. Both parents became involved with substance misuse services.

Sue and Lee set five clear goals:

1   Attending counselling sessions.

2   Baby Rose did not miss or arrive late for appointments.

3   Not to drink more than they had planned they should.

4   To avoid getting into arguments.

5   To learn and practise communication skills.

This family achieved all five goals during the four week intervention. They found the concept of setting goals so useful that they had set new ones for themselves when I made a follow up visit.

> *(Worker) really listened to us . . . our relationship is a lot stronger . . . I would recommend this service to anybody . . . if it wasn't for this service we would have lost our baby . . . we know what is expected of us now, the therapist explained it really well.*
>
> Sue and Lee in a core group meeting

Rick and Julie

Rick and Julie had four children. The youngest was two years old and the oldest was fifteen. The two middle children of eight and twelve were not attending school and all were missing health appointments. The family were very short of money and the childcare team had numerous referrals from neighbours because the children were wandering the street late at night. There was little food in the house, the team had put the children's names on the CPR and were considering the need to remove them.

With the help of their worker, the family explored their hopes and dreams for the future. They created a clear and detailed picture of a possible future that had all the children at home, developing and growing so that they optimised their chances of happiness and success. Both parents wanted to work or study to improve their prospects. This image gave us the basis of a clear plan and gave the family hope that things could get better.

We together looked at the steps that would enable their 'dream' to be achieved and within four weeks the children had returned to school, the parents had taken responsibility for structuring their appointments and they were taking action to deal with their finances. They were able to spend money on things they needed like food and clothing.

We did this through building hope, exploring solutions such as using calendars, debt reduction skills, and ways of negotiating with the children.

Six months later the older children were de-registered. A year later the case was closed to children's services.

Rick and Julie set four goals:

1   The two middle children to go to school each day.

2   To use a calendar.

3   To keep all appointments with professionals.

4   To deal with debt.

> *Very helpful, since (the therapist) has been involved with us we've kept all of our appointments and the children haven't missed a day off school.*
> Julie and Rick on a service evaluation form

Linda

Linda had three children, the youngest was two years old and the oldest was seven. The seven year old had been sexually abused by a friend of the family. Linda had problems controlling her anger and had hit her youngest child. Other people used her house to use drugs. A great deal of the household income was diverted into drugs and much of her social circle consisted of users and dealers, her family all used amphetamines. She said that she didn't know any 'normal people'. Childcare professionals were concerned for the children. Linda considered herself to be 'worthless', 'ugly' and 'stupid'. She had been abused and robbed by a variety of short term boyfriends.

We spent time looking at her strengths, her house was always immaculate, she had a creative flair and enjoyed decorating. When she was available for her children she was a loving mother and set boundaries to her children's behaviour that were appropriate and promoted their development, neither too lax nor too controlling. However, at other times she was aggressive and dismissive towards her children.

We did the miracle question, explored Linda's dreams. Her dream was to get drugs and drug users out of her home completely, she wanted to take control of her home and to learn to be a better parent. She wanted to help her children to develop into confident happy people who are proud of their mother and she wanted to learn new skills that would help her to feel more relaxed, more in control, calmer and more predictable. We taught her relaxation skills, assertiveness skills, new ways of communicating with the children and managing their behaviour. Exploring her strengths gave her the confidence to talk about her dream of going to college, meeting a new circle of people and changing her lifestyle. With our support she enrolled in a summer school in woodcarving. She was very successful and plans to go onto a long term course in aromatherapy. We supported her with referrals to the Community Addictions Unit and she was prescribed a substitute for her amphetamines. A year later she was no longer spending on drugs, and is reducing her substitute. This case was later closed to children's services.

I saw her about two years after working with her, I was at a stunt show with my children and she walked past me with her partner and children, looking happy. She didn't see me.

Linda set three clear goals:

1   To be able to take control in her own home. To stop drugs from coming into the house.

2   To focus on helping her children to develop into confident, happy people who are proud of their mother.

3   To learn and use to new skills that will help her to become more relaxed, more in control, calmer and more predictable.

> *(worker) has helped me to become the person that I want to be, not the person that I would have become, a druggie, hopeless, lost my kids and everything . . . I think (worker) is brill.*
>
> Linda on a service evaluation form

Of course anybody could have made the referral to the addiction services but I doubt whether Linda would have gone to the appointment, her feelings of self worth were so low that she would most likely have been talked out of it by the drug users who used the house. What actually did the trick in this case was the assertiveness work done with Linda in her home and the daily encouragement of her to practice. Being available every day to encourage her, talking about her fears and helping her to come up with strategies to deal with particular people helped her to get rid of the drug users and dealers from her and her children's home.

Continued improvement

Throughout this intervention we are building on people's problem solving skills. Most often we do this through modelling, sometimes through exploring their strengths and sometimes through formal teaching methods including one to one work, homework and handouts. When people learn new things they become more resilient. Knowing that they have learned something gives them the confidence to learn more, they know they can change and adapt and so it becomes a little easier for them to deal with crises when they come along. People adapt their new skills to different situations, it is not unusual to teach 'I' messages to a client to use with her sister and find later on that she is using them on her son, husband and father too. People become stronger. This work builds confidence and self esteem, it makes people feel good about the things they are successful at rather than failures for the things they fail at.

We find that when we visit families during the year following the intervention to measure peoples goal attainment, they have continued to improve for about six months after we have left and they are usually still at that level at our one year follow up. If people are having trouble in that time they, or the referrer can contact us to provide a 'booster' session. We will work with the family for a short period to work on new skills or practice old ones.

Most parents who are having trouble with social services know what they want, and I often hear people saying things like, 'I want us to be a 'normal' family', 'I want us to be happy together', 'I want to stop drinking or I want the drinking to stop affecting my children', 'I want the pain to go away'.

What people often lack is the confidence that they can do it, the skills or resources to help them to do it and the self esteem that makes people feel that it is worth the effort. Sometimes we have to work quite hard just to get the client to the point where they will say, 'I just want us to be a happy family together.'

Many of us suffer from existence pain at one time or another. Our clients are generally poor, generally under-educated, often the victims of crime and other abuse and rarely able to see real light at the end of the tunnel other than a lottery win. They suffer from more existence pain than most. Speaking from anger and frustration is often the only position of strength many people feel they have. The only way they can feel strong is by asserting themselves, the only way they can appear powerful, feel counted, have some sense of importance or even validity in the world, is by shouting, being abusive, by swearing at their kids and telling them that they wish they had never been born. Some people deal with lack of self-worth by showing strength by damaging things or people, by taking other peoples things, and by flashy ostentatious displays of property. But most live lives of quiet desperation.

We try to teach people a different kind of strength, a deeper strength that says: 'I can do it, I am strong, I can hear and understand your needs and your frustrations and I can still show you love'.

Summary

No one is comfortable when they begin the journey from the known to the unknown, but we can be comforted by the knowledge that the summit is not really new. We are not leaving home; we are coming home.

Lance Secretan, *Reclaiming Higher Ground* (1997)

This final section of the manual I would like to structure as a quick and easy reminder of the stages of a brief intervention using this model.

Take the referral

- Complete referral form from info supplied by referrer (negotiate goalposts).

- If referral seems appropriate and you have space, inform your colleague of name and address of your new client so they may be able to make sure that you are safe.

- Open a client file.

- Within 24 hours of referral make contact with client.

Week One

- Visit and engage family.

- Be polite and wait to be invited in, to sit down. Listen and observe – allow client to safely express their anger, frustration, fear etc. Explore concerns which family brings up. Explore concerns in referral form. Establish what the family wants it to look like when better. Reflect positives. Provide honest and respectful feedback. Build a relationship with the family based on positive regard and hope. Make sure the family makes the decisions.

- Aim to be invited back.

- Bring leaflets. Does the family want the service? Explain why referral was made – share contents of referral form.

- Reinforce positives.

Make assessment

- Does the family fit referral criteria? Is the family in crisis – do they feel the need to make changes, if not can you motivate them?

- Can the children be conditionally safe during the intervention?

- Is the person actively engaged in the process?

- Assess the level of motivation to make changes (scaling question – how important is it from one to ten).

- Assess the family's sense of their own ability to make changes. (Scaling question 'How confident are you on a scale of one to ten, that you can make the changes').

- Assess society, community, family and individual factors.

- Reinforce positives.

Are family aware of the facts?

- Do they know what a social worker means when they say 'the authority will have to take legal advice'?

- Do they understand what a Child Protection Case Conference is and what its powers are?

- Do they understand the powers of the local authority?

- Reinforce positives.

- Fill in referral and assessment statistics form and give to admin:
  - ☐ Working agreement with family.
  - ☐ Give family a case file of their own.
  - ☐ Devise safety plan with family.
  - ☐ Feedback to the referrer.

- 72 hour report.

- Safety plan.

- Reinforce positives.

- Working agreement.

Week Two

- Explore the family values and feed these back, validating peoples' beliefs, exploring dangerous beliefs, creating a cognitive dissonance and finding resources that will help people change.

- Explore family and individual strengths validating and building on peoples' strengths, and finding resources that will help people change.

- Help the family to develop ideas about change, negotiating goals and priorities.

- Help family to devise and scale goal sheets using the clients' language, strengths and beliefs and create an expectation of change. Clients have complete ownership of the goals. These goals describe clear and observable behavioural change.

- Devise a weekly plan which focusses on each goal and each individual and which sets clear tasks for the remainder of the intervention. This needs to have been done before the end of Week Two.

- Overcome any barriers to learning. You may have been helping clients to learn how to meet basic needs.

- Reinforce positives.

Week Three and Four

- Using goals sheets and Weekly Plan, teach family members new skills, ideas and ways of thinking that will help them on their way to achieving the goals they have set, exploring new ideas, revisiting old coping strategies, teaching new skills and evaluating.

- Practice, practice, practice.

- Reinforce positives.

End of Week Four

- Score goal sheets again.

- Write report and give to client and referrer. Include evaluation feedback forms (see Appendix).

- Hold maintenance meeting.

- Reinforce positives.

- Complete Closure Statistics form for admin (see Appendix).

- End Intervention.

- Follow up and re-score goals after one, three, six and twelve months.

- Do short 'booster' sessions with family if requested by family or referrer.

- Complete follow up statistics forms for admin.

Appendix

Through the manual you will find examples of some of the forms we use. This section holds a clean set for you to use or modify to suit your needs.

Contents

- **Referral Form** – used by therapist, kept on client file and copy given to client.

- **Referral and Assessment Statistics Form** – filled in by therapist and given to admin for data collection.

- **Agreement** – written agreement between therapist and family.

- **Goal Sheet** – used by therapist and family, kept on client file, copy given to client.

- **Closure Statistics Form** – filled in by therapist and handed to admin for data collection – these statistics forms are used to track families' progress following closure and over the next 12 months.

- **Follow up Statistics Form** – see above.

- **Social Worker Feedback Form** – sent to referrer with closing report.

- **Client Feedback Form** – given to client with closing report.

Referral Form

Client number: _____   Referral date: _____

Family name: _____

Address: _____

Telephone: _____

Is the family aware of this referral?   Yes ☐   No ☐

Family structure or genogram:

Name	DoB/Age	Relationship	Employment/ School	Address and Phone	Ethnicity

Child's social worker: _____

Team: _____   Telephone: _____

Reason for referral:

- ▣ Are there child protection issues related to substance misuse?
- ▣ Is there a risk of registration or accommodation if no changes are made?
- ▣ Is the risk immediate?
- ▣ If not immediate, do the family say they are in crisis and recognise the need for change?

Referrer's/family's expectations of outcome of this intervention:

Current legal status: _____

Care Order ☐   CPR ☐   Other ☐ (please specify)

Neglect ☐   Sexual abuse ☐

Physical harm ☐   Emotional abuse ☐

Other professionals involved:

Do any of the family members have any special needs or requirements?

Risk assessment: Yes ☐   No ☐

Details:

Type of referral: ☐   Immediate risk ☐   Future risk

Allocated worker: Name:

☐ No space – Case closed

☐ Inappropriate referral

Reason for inappropriateness:

Referral and Assessment Statistics Form

Date of referral: _____   Case number: _____

Referral agency: _____

Family details:

Number of children referred:	under 3	11–14
	3–6 over	14
	7–10	

Adult carers referred	Mother	Partner
(circle as many as apply):	Father	Grandparent
	Step parent	Other (please specify)

Crisis: Immediate risk of accommodating children
(please circle)   Immediate risk of registering children on Child Protection Register
                  Other (specify)
                  None

Legal status: Children on Child Protection Register   Yes   No
(Please circle)

If registered, category of registration	Neglect	Sexual abuse
	Physical harm	Emotional abuse
	Care Orders	Yes No

Outcome of referral: Inappropriate referral – case closed
(please circle)   Appropriate referral – no spaces
                       Case allocated for assessment

Assessment:

Date case allocated: _____

Initial appointment within one working day?   Yes   No (specify)

Risk behaviour:	Substance misuse	Domestic violence
(Circle all that apply)	Neglect	Parenting skills
	Physical abuse	Mental health of carer
	Sexual abuse	Other (specify)

Outcome of	Ongoing involvement	Unable to engage family
assessment:	Family refused service	Referrer refused service
(Please circle)	Family moved away	Other (specify)

Unable to make children conditionally safe CLOSED

Agreement

Your four weeks of work start today because you say you want to make some changes in your life to keep your family together. Your Therapist is _____.Their job is to help you to make those changes. At the end of four weeks they will write to the social worker and tell them what you have changed about your life. You will be given a copy of all written information that your worker shares with social workers.

This is an agreement between you and the other members of your family and between those people and your worker.

I agree that . . .

1   I agree to contact my worker and inform them if I cannot make an appointment and need to change it.

2   It is important for me and for my family that I try different ways of doing things and make some changes. I want my family to stay together. So I will personally make some changes in my life so that *we can* stay together.

3   I want the children to have a life that gives them the skills, the emotional support and the protection they need for a successful and happy future.

4   Our worker will share information with other professionals if required so that working together they can provide the right help to help me keep my children safe. This information will be about the effect of my lifestyle and drug or alcohol use on my children. What my family need help with, what is causing problems and what I am doing well at.

5   The welfare of my children is the most important thing, if the worker is concerned about the safety of my children, they will inform the childcare social worker whether I agree or not.

Signed:

_____   _____

_____   _____

_____   _____

                                            Date: _____

Working with _____ start today

Goal Sheet

Family name: _____   **Therapist:** _____

Goal No. _____

Statement of problem:
(*This statement must be behaviourally specific to what was observed or reported*)

Date goal scaled: _____   **Date when scored:** _____

Rating when scaled: _____   **Rating when scored:** _____

Who's goal: _____   **Weight:** _____
                                            (10 being most important, 0 being least important)

Most unfavourable outcome thought likely:
(−**2**)

Less than expected level of success:
(−**1**)

On target – Expected level of success:
(**0**)

More than expected level of success:
(+**1**)

Best anticipated success:
(+**2**)

Closure Statistics Form

Date of closure: _____   **Case number:** _____

Contact details: Number of weeks: ____   Hours of face to face contact: ____

Number of callouts: ____   phone ____   face to face ____

Number of goals:

Goal #1
Rating when scaled	−2	−1	0	+1	+2
Rating on closure	−2	−1	0	+1	+2

Goal #2
Rating when scaled	−2	−1	0	+1	+2
Rating on closure	−2	−1	0	+1	+2

Goal #3
Rating when scaled	−2	−1	0	+1	+2
Rating on closure	−2	−1	0	+1	+2

Goal #4
Rating when scaled	−2	−1	0	+1	+2
Rating on closure	−2	−1	0	+1	+2

Goal #5
Rating when scaled	−2	−1	0	+1	+2
Rating on closure	−2	−1	0	+1	+2

Goal #6
Rating when scaled	−2	−1	0	+1	+2
Rating on closure	−2	−1	0	+1	+2

Reason for closure:

Planned ending: (Moves to review procedure)
Family refused service before planned ending
Further incident of abuse – not conditionally safe
Family moved away – No further Option 2 involvement
Referrer finished involvement
Children accommodated
Other (please specify)

Significant changes:

Children placed on Child Protection Register	Yes	No
Children de-registered	Yes	No
Children accommodated	Yes	No
Case closed to children's services	Yes	No
Other	Yes	No

Follow Up Statistics Form

1 month/3 months/6 months/1 year (Delete inappropriate)

Date of follow up: _____   **Case number:** _____

Number of goals:

Goal #1

| Rating on closure | −2 | −1 | 0 | +1 | +2 |
| Rating on follow up | −2 | −1 | 0 | +1 | +2 |

Goal #2

| Rating on closure | −2 | −1 | 0 | +1 | +2 |
| Rating on follow up | −2 | −1 | 0 | +1 | +2 |

Goal #3

| Rating on closure | −2 | −1 | 0 | +1 | +2 |
| Rating on follow up | −2 | −1 | 0 | +1 | +2 |

Goal #4

| Rating on closure | −2 | −1 | 0 | +1 | +2 |
| Rating on follow up | −2 | −1 | 0 | +1 | +2 |

Goal #5

| Rating on closure | −2 | −1 | 0 | +1 | +2 |
| Rating on follow up | −2 | −1 | 0 | +1 | +2 |

Goal #6

| Rating on closure | −2 | −1 | 0 | +1 | +2 |
| Rating on follow up | −2 | −1 | 0 | +1 | +2 |

Significant changes:

Children placed on Child Protection Register	Yes	No
Children de-registered	Yes	No
Children accommodated	Yes	No
Case closed to children's services	Yes	No
Other	Yes	No

No follow up possible:

1 Family refused follow up
2 Family moved away
3 Unable to contact family
4 Other (please specify

Entered:

Social Worker's Feedback Form

Now that our work with this family is over we would like to find out what you thought of our intervention. This is your opportunity to tell us what did and what didn't work for you, as well as your feelings about what worked for this family. Your comments will help us to improve the service and make it more useful to other families. Please tick the boxes and make any comments you think would be helpful.

Date: _____ Family name: _____

Therapist's name: _____ Social worker's name: _____

1. How well did you get along with the therapist?

Very poorly ☐   Poorly ☐   OK ☐   Well ☐   Very well ☐

2. Was it helpful to you, knowing that this family could call a therapist in an emergency?

Yes ☐   No ☐   Didn't know they could ☐

3. What *useful* work did this family do with the therapist?

_____

_____

4. Has this family adopted new *skills*, *behaviours* or *beliefs* that help them in their parenting?

Yes ☐   No ☐   Don't know ☐   Please explain: ☐

_____

_____

5. What could the therapist have done that might have been more helpful for this family?

_____

_____

6. What did the therapist do that was useful to YOU as a worker?

_____

_____

7. What could the therapist have done that would have been more helpful to YOU?

_____

_____

Many thanks for taking the time to fill out this form.

Your effort will help to improve the service for other workers and families.

Client Feedback Form

Now that the intensive work with your family is over, we would like to find out what you thought of it. This is your opportunity to tell us what worked for you, and what didn't. Your comments will help us to make the service better and more useful to other families. Please tick the boxes and make any comments you think would help.

Date: _____   Family name: _____   Therapist's name: _____

1. How well did you get along with your therapist?
☐ Very poorly   ☐ Poorly ☐   OK ☐ Well   ☐ Very well

2. Was it helpful knowing that you could call your therapist?
☐ Yes   ☐ No   ☐ Didn't know I could

3. What USEFUL things did your family work on with your therapist?
a. _____
b. _____
c. _____

4. What were the most MEMORABLE things your therapist did with your family?
a. _____
b. _____
c. _____

5. Have you continued to use the skills you learned?
Not at all ☐   Sometimes ☐   Quite a lot ☐

6. How helpful has this been for your family?
☐ Very unhelpful   ☐ Unhelpful   ☐ Made no difference
☐ Helpful   ☐ Very helpful   Please explain:

_____

_____

7. Is there anything your therapist could have done that might have been more helpful?
No ☐   Yes ☐   If so, what would have been more helpful?

_____

_____

8. Would you recommend this service to another family in a similar situation?
No ☐   Yes ☐

9. How could the service be improved?

_____

_____

Many thanks for taking the time to fill out this form.

Your effort will help to improve the service for other families.

Useful Contacts

National Coalition for Child Protection Reform. Papers on Family Preservation Services.
http://www.nccpr.org/

Research on Family Preservation and Reunification Programs
http://aspe.hhs.gov/hsp/cyp/fplitrev.htm

The Brief Therapy Practice offer training in Solution Focused Brief Therapy, 7–8 Newbury Street, London EC1A 7HU.
Tel: 020 7600 3366
Fax: 020 7600 3388
Email: *solutions@brieftherapy.org.uk*

Option 2 runs training courses for professionals wishing to use this model.
Contact: Rhoda Emlyn-Jones, House 54, Cardiff Royal Infirmary, Newport Road, Cardiff CF24 0SZ.
Tel: 02920 468 555/6
Email: *R.Emlyn-Jones@cardiff.gov.uk*
http://www.option2.org

Mark Hamer
http://www.another-way.co.uk

Further Reading

Altstein, H. and McRoy, R. (2000) *Does Family Preservation Serve a Child's Best Interests?* Georgetown University Press.

Bannister, A., Barrett, K. and Shearer, E. (1990) *Listening to Children: The Professional Response to Hearing the Abused Child.* Chichester, NSPCC/John Wiley and Sons.

Berg, I.K. (1991) *Family Preservation: A Brief Therapy Workbook.* London, BT Press.

Berg, I.K. and Kelly, S. (2000) *Building Solutions in Child Protective Services.* New York, Norton.

Bloom, B.L. (1992) *Planned Short-term Psychotherapy: A Clinical Handbook.* Boston, Allyn and Bacon.

Braye, S. and Preston-Shoot, M. (1995) *Empowering Practice in Social Care.* Buckingham, OU Press.

Burgess, A.W. and Baldwin, B.A. (1981) *Crisis Intervention, Theory and Practice.* New Jersey, Prentice Hall.

Butler, I. and Williamson, H. (1994) *Children Speak: Children, Trauma and Social Work.* Essex, Longman.

Campion, M.J. (1995) *Who's Fit to be a Parent?* London, Routledge.

Cannan, C. and Warren, C. (1997) *Social Action with Children and Families: A Community Development Approach to Child and Family Welfare.* London, Routledge.

Canter, L. and Canter, M. (1988) *Assertive Discipline for Parents.* New York. Harper and Row.

Cleaver, H., Unell, I. and Aldgate, J. (1999) *Children's Needs – Parenting Capacity: The Impact of Parental Mental Illness, Problem Alcohol and Drug Use, and Domestic Violence on Children's Development.* DoH.

Cooper, A., Hetherington, R. and Katz, I. (2003) *The Risk Factor, Making the Child Protection System Work for Children.* London, Demos.

Dartington Social Research Unit (2004) *Refocussing Children's Services Towards Prevention: Lessons from the literature.* Department for Education and Skills.

Dattilio, F.M. and Freeman, A. (Eds.) (2000) *Cognitive Behavioural Strategies in Crisis Intervention.* New York, The Guilford Press.

Doel, M. and Marsh, P. (1992) *Task Centred Social Work.* Aldershot, Arena, Ashgate Publishing.

Eysenk, H.J. (1966) *The Effects of Psychotherapy.* New York, International Science Press.

Fischer, J. (1978) *Effective Casework Practice: An Eclectic Approach.* New York, McGraw Hill.

Garfield, S. (1989) *The Practice of Brief Psychotherapy.* New York, Pergamon Press.

Griffin, E. (1997) *A First Look at Communication Theory.* New York, McGraw Hill.

Harbin, F. and Murphy, M. (Eds.) (2000) *Substance Misuse and Child Care: How to Understand, Assist and Intervene when Drugs Affect Parenting.* Lyme Regis, Russell House Publishing.

HM Government (2003) *Every Child Matters.* London, HMSO.

Kiresuk, T. and Lund, S.H. (1976) Process and Outcome Measurement Using Goal Attainment Scaling. In Glass, G. (Ed.) *Evaluation Studies: Review Annual.* Beverley Hills, Sage Publications.

Kinney, J., Haapala D. and Booth, C. (1991) *Keeping Families Together: The Homebuilders Model.* New York, Aldine De Gruyter.

Kroll, B. and Taylor, A. (2003) *Parental Substance Misuse and Child Welfare.* London, Jessica Kingsley.

Lishman, J. (1994) *Communication in Social Work.* London, Macmillan.

Macdonald, G. and Williamson, E. (2002) *Against the Odds: An Evaluation of Child and Family Support Services.* London, National Children's Bureau.

McMahon, A. (1988) *Damned If You Do, Damned If You Don't: Working in Child Welfare.* Aldershot, Ashgate.

Miller, W.R. and Rollnick, S. (1991) *Motivational Interviewing: Preparing People to Change Addictive Behavior.* New York, Guilford Press.

Neenan, M. and Dryden, W. (2000) *Essential Cognitive Therapy.* London, Whurr Publishers.

Parad, H.J. and Parad L.G. (1990) *Crisis Intervention: The Practitioners Sourcebook for Brief Therapy.* Milwaukee, Family Service Association of America.

Roberts, A.R. (1990) *Crisis Intervention Handbook: Assessment, Treatment and Research.* Belmont CA, Wadsworth.

Roberts, A.R. (Ed.) (1995) *Crisis Intervention and Time-Limited Cognitive Treatment.* London, Sage.

Rogers, C.R. (1961) *On Becoming a Person: A Therapist's View of Psychotherapy.* Boston, Houghton Mifflin.

Scott, J., Williams, J., Mark, G. and Beck, A.T. (Eds.) (1989) *Cognitive Therapy in Clinical Practice.* London, Routledge.

Stevenson, O. (1998) *Neglected Children, Issues and Dilemmas.* Oxford, Blackwell Science.

Velleman, R. and Orford, J. (1999) *Risk and Resilience: Adults who were the Children of Problem Drinkers.* Amsterdam, Harwood Academic Publishers.